Problem-Solving in Mathematics

RANDALL I. CHARLES

FRANK K. LESTER, JR.

ANNE M. BLOOMER

Contributing Writer

VICKIE K. DORIS

TEACHER SOURCEBOOK

GRADE 2

Innovative Learning Publications

Addison-Wesley Publishing Company

Menlo Park, California • Reading, Massachusetts • New York
Don Mills, Ontario • Wokingham, England • Amsterdam
Bonn • Paris • Milan • Madrid • Sydney • Singapore
Tokyo • Seoul • Taipei • Mexico City • San Juan

Managing Editor: Cathy Anderson
Project Editor: Mali Apple
Production: Leanne Collins
Design Manager: Jeff Kelly
Text and Cover Design: Christy Butterfield
Illustrations: Joan Holub
Jane McCreary
Masami Miyamoto
Margaret Sanfilippo

This book is published by Innovative Learning Publications™, an imprint of Addison-Wesley's Alternative Publishing Group.

The blackline masters in this publication are designed to be used with appropriate duplicating equipment to reproduce copies for classroom use. Addison-Wesley Publishing Company grants permission to classroom teachers to reproduce these masters.

Copyright © 1996, 1985 by Addison-Wesley Publishing Company, Inc. Printed in the United States of America.

ISBN 0-201-49362-4

5 6 7 8 9 10 ML 04 03 02 01 00

This book is printed on recycled stock.

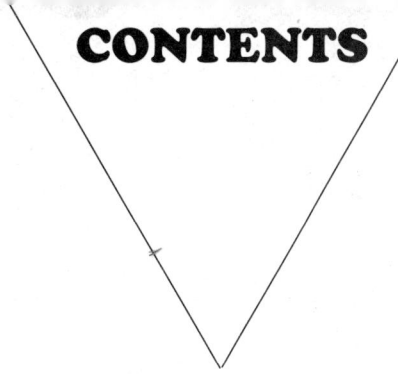

CONTENTS

Overview

Goals of the Program   v
Organization of the Program   v
Building a Positive Classroom Climate   vii
The Teacher's Role   viii
Cooperative Learning for Problem Solving   xii
Using Manipulatives   xiii
Assessing Students   xiii
Some Special Considerations   xiv

Problem Sets

SET 1	FIRE STATION NUMBER 1 1		**SET 15**	PONY RIDES 85
SET 2	INSECTS IN THE GARDEN 7		**SET 16**	A SPECIAL PIG 91
SET 3	BUTTERFLIES AND FLOWERS 13		**SET 17**	ROOM 7 97
SET 4	THE OAKDALE EARTH SAVERS 19		**SET 18**	THE IMAGINARY FARM 103
SET 5	GUINEA PIG PETS 25		**SET 19**	WINTER FUN 109
SET 6	THE SCAVENGER HUNT 31		**SET 20**	DAVY CROCKETT 115
SET 7	AT THE ROLLER RINK 37		**SET 21**	EDUARDO'S COLLECTION 121
SET 8	THE POST OFFICE 43		**SET 22**	PICNIC IN THE PARK 127
SET 9	FUTURE DREAMS 49		**SET 23**	MAILING A LETTER 135
SET 10	JOHNNY APPLESEED 55		**SET 24**	DETECTIVE DONNA 143
SET 11	SUMMER FRIENDS 61		**SET 25**	ALL KINDS OF TRAINS 151
SET 12	LIFE AT A POND 67		**SET 26**	A DOG'S LIFE 159
SET 13	THE ANIMAL SHELTER 73		**SET 27**	RALPH THE SUPERCHICKEN 165
SET 14	LEARNING TO ICE SKATE 79		**SET 28**	SCHOOL CARNIVAL 173

Assessment Appendix   179

OVERVIEW

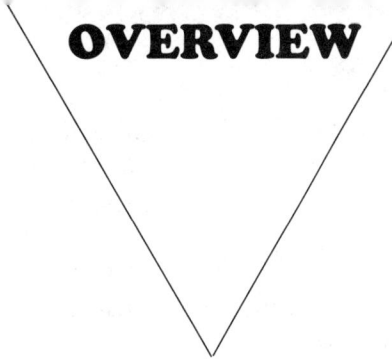

"The importance of problem solving to all education cannot be overestimated. To serve this goal effectively, the mathematics curriculum must provide many opportunities for all students to meet the problems that interest and challenge them and that, with appropriate effort, they can solve."
—NCTM Standards, 1989

Problem-Solving Experiences in Mathematics (PSEM) provides the kinds of opportunities described in the NCTM Standards and is designed to supplement any instructional program. It consists of 120 problem-solving experiences grouped by story themes and a teaching strategy for problem solving. A separate package of blackline masters provides students with support material.

PSEM was designed with the NCTM Standards in mind.

Goals of the Program

The ultimate goal of any problem-solving program is to improve students' performance at solving problems correctly. Although this is the ultimate goal, instructional goals need to be more specific and developmental. The goals of PSEM are to

1. Improve students' willingness to try problems and improve their perseverance when solving problems.
2. Improve students' self-concepts with respect to their abilities to solve problems.
3. Make students aware of problem-solving strategies.
4. Make students aware of the value of approaching problems in a systematic manner.
5. Make students aware that many problems can be solved in more than one way, including with the use of manipulatives.
6. Improve students' abilities to select appropriate solution strategies.
7. Improve students' abilities to implement solution strategies accurately.
8. Improve students' abilities to monitor and evaluate their thinking while solving problems.
9. Improve students' abilities to get more correct answers to problems.
10. Improve students' abilities to communicate their thinking.

Organization of the Program

There are four types of problem-solving experiences in this program: problem-solving readiness activities, problem-solving skill activities, one-step problems, and process problems. The 120 experiences in this book are grouped into 28 sets. Each set begins with an introductory story that provides a unifying theme for the experiences in that set.

Problem sets are built around real-world themes.

PSEM provides a problem-solving experience—120 in all—for almost every day of the school year. The problems were selected and sequenced so the concepts and skills needed to solve each problem would have been introduced to students approximately two months before they are encountered here, *if* the teacher follows the scope and sequence of lessons in most textbooks. For problems at the beginning of the year, concepts and skills are limited to those most students should have encountered prior to second grade. This organization means that students' work is limited to a *review* of concepts and skills. The emphasis on problem-solving instruction can thus be on understanding problems, selecting and implementing appropriate solution strategies, and checking one's work, rather than on carrying out computational skills.

PROBLEM-SOLVING READINESS ACTIVITIES are experiences designed to prepare students for future problem-solving experiences by building their confidence in dealing with real-world situations that involve numbers. Six types of readiness activities are included in Grade 2:

1. Tell how numbers are used in the real world.
2. Given a story, answer questions about information in the story.
3. Tell a story using a given number.
4. Given a story, visualize objects and action in the story.
5. Given a number story, retell the story changing the numbers or the setting.
6. Given a story, act out the action in the story.

PROBLEM-SOLVING SKILL ACTIVITIES are experiences designed to promote the development of thinking processes involved in problem solving. Seven types of skill activities are included in Grade 2:

1. Given a number story, tell a question that can be answered using data in the story.
2. Given a picture, choose/tell a questions whose answer would be found by using addition/subtraction.
3. Given a story problem and the start of a picture, complete the picture to match the story problem.
4. Given the story problem with missing data, choose/tell appropriate data for solving the problem.
5. Given a story problem, tell whether addition or subtraction is needed to find the solution.
6. Given the story problem with missing data, choose/tell appropriate data for solving the problem.
7. Given a story problem, tell whether addition or subtraction is needed to find the solution.

Problem-solving readiness and skill activities build a foundation for problem solving.

PROCESS PROBLEMS are problems that cannot be solved by simply choosing an operation. Instead, process problems are solved using one or more of these strategies:

1. Guess and check
2. Draw a picture
3. Make an organized list
4. Make a table, chart, or graph
5. Look for a pattern
6. Use logical reasoning
7. Use manipulatives

Because process problems cannot be solved by simply choosing an operation, they exemplify and provide practice with the thinking processes inherent in problem solving. The following chart indicates the strategies that can be used to solve the process problems in this book. The chart does not show all of the possible ways of solving the problems—only those that are most commonly used. Also, manipulatives can be used with any of the strategies; their use is incorporated within all of the strategies.

Process problems exemplify and provide practice with the thinking processes inherent in problem solving.

LIKELY STRATEGIES USED IN THE PROCESS PROBLEMS

GUESS AND CHECK
7–8, 31–32, 56, 68, 80, 90, 105, 120

DRAW A PICTURE
19–20, 27, 43–44, 51–52, 63, 75, 84–85, 99–100, 114

MAKE AN ORGANIZED LIST
3–4, 7, 27–28, 55, 67, 79, 89, 104, 119

MAKE A TABLE, CHART, OR GRAPH
15–16, 39–40, 59, 71, 94, 109, 115

LOOK FOR A PATTERN
11–12, 15–16, 35–36, 39–40, 59–60, 71–72, 76, 94–95, 109–110, 115

USE LOGICAL REASONING
7, 19–20, 23–24, 31, 43–44, 47–48, 51–52, 56, 63–64, 75, 84–85, 90, 100, 104, 114

The two process problems in sets 1 through 12 are matched by probable solution strategies to enable you to teach students how to use problem-solving strategies. Even though the process problems are matched within each of these sets, *it is very important that students are not forced to use the strategy suggested by the hint. In fact, students should be encouraged to find solutions to problems using as many different strategies as they can.*

The process problems in Grade 2 are organized in the following manner.

ORGANIZATION OF THE PROCESS PROBLEMS

SET 1 MAKE/COMPLETE AN ORGANIZED LIST

SET 2 GUESS AND CHECK

SET 3 LOOK FOR A PATTERN

SET 4 COMPLETE A TABLE

SET 5 USE A PICTURE

SET 6 USE LOGICAL REASONING

} The two process problems in each of sets 1–6 are those most students will solve using the strategy shown at the left.

SET 7 COMPLETE AN ORGANIZED LIST

SET 8 GUESS AND CHECK

SET 9 LOOK FOR A PATTERN

SET 10 COMPLETE A TABLE

SET 11 USE/DRAW A PICTURE

SET 12 USE LOGICAL REASONING

} The two process problems in each of sets 7–12 are still grouped by the most probable solution strategy.

SETS 13–28

} The two process problems in each of sets 13–28 are mixed. That is, students would most likely not use the same solution strategy on each.

Building a Positive Classroom Climate

In the first two months of the school year, the most important goal with regard to problem solving should be to establish a positive classroom climate. Then, you can begin to focus on the development of the students' problem-solving abilities. The importance of a positive classroom climate cannot be overemphasized in building a successful problem-solving program.

> *In the first two months of the school year, establish a positive classroom climate.*

Many factors affect classroom climate. Among the most important are the appropriateness of the content (not too difficult and not too easy), the teacher's evaluation practices, and the teacher's attitude and actions related to problem solving. Of these, the teacher's attitude and actions are most important. Here are some things that will help you establish a positive climate in your classroom for problem solving:

- Be enthusiastic about problem solving.
- Have students bring in problems from their personal experiences.
- Personalize problems whenever possible (e.g., use students' names).
- Recognize and reinforce willingness and perseverance.
- Reward risk takers.
- Encourage students to play hunches.
- Accept unusual solutions.
- Praise students for getting correct solutions, but during problem solving, emphasize the selection and use of problem-solving strategies.
- Emphasize persistence rather than speed.

The Teacher's Role

All of the problem-solving experiences in this book were designed to be given orally, with the teacher playing an active role leading the students through each experience.

USING THE BLACKLINE MASTERS Many of the problem-solving experiences in this book are accompanied by a blackline master (BLM). BLMs provide support material for the problem-solving experiences; *they are not worksheets to be assigned to students.* BLMs can be used only as part of the teacher-oriented, oral problem-solving experiences. A sample BLM for a process problem is shown here. The students should have a copy of each BLM.

USING THE INTRODUCTORY STORIES These stories provide a unifying theme for all of the problem-solving experiences in a set. Each story has an accompanying BLM to be distributed to the students. The stories are to be read by the teacher as the students look at the BLM. The discussion questions given in the teacher notes can be interspersed throughout the reading of the story or can all be asked after the story has been read. The questions do not require mathematics to be answered. Instead, they help familiarize students with the theme, promote the improvement of students' listening skills, and promote the development of students' creativity. The introductory story and discussion questions also serve to motivate students for the problem-solving experiences in the set that follows. If you use a "problem-of-the-day" approach for this program, the introductory story could be read and discussed on Monday and the follow-up problem-solving experiences used on the remaining four days of the week.

USING THE LESSON PLAN FOR PROBLEM-SOLVING READINESS AND SKILL ACTIVITIES The lesson plan for readiness and skill activities consists of recommended teaching actions specific to each activity. A sample activity is shown here. The teaching actions provide guidelines for how to (orally) introduce the activity and lead students through a discussion of the activity.

---

65 Skill Activity

Tell the Operation

PROBLEM A
There were 9 boys and 7 girls in Ms. Nomura's class on Monday. How many more boys than girls were in Ms. Nomura's class on Monday?

PROBLEM B
On Ms. Nomura's bulletin board, there are __ jobs that need to be done in the morning and __ jobs that need to be done in the afternoon. What is the total number of jobs that need to be done in Room 7?

PROBLEM C
Ms. Nomura told __ of the students to clean their desks. So far, only __ of them have done their job. How many more still have to clean their desk?

Note: Problem B is an addition situation. Problem C is a missing-addend subtraction situation.

TEACHING ACTIONS

1. Read Problem A. Have students tell the operation they would use to solve the problem. Do not have them solve it. Discuss their choice.
2. Tell students you are going to read another story, but now you are going to leave out the numbers. Read Problem B, and have students tell the operation they would use to solve it. Discuss why.
3. Repeat Teaching Action 2 for problem C.

USING THE LESSON PLAN FOR PROCESS PROBLEMS AND ONE-STEP PROBLEMS The lesson plan for each process problem and one-step problem is outlined as in the sample shown. Next to each section of the lesson plan are general teaching actions recommended for problem solving. The table on page xi gives a complete description of the teaching actions and describes the purpose of each.

TEACHING ACTIONS BEFORE

1. Read the problem.
2. Ask questions for understanding the problem.
3. Discuss possible solution strategies.

TEACHING ACTIONS DURING

4. Observe students.
5. Give hints as needed for solving the problem.
6. Require students to check back and answer the problem.
7. Give problem extension(s) as needed.

TEACHING ACTIONS AFTER

8. Discuss solution(s).
9. Discuss related problem(s) and extension(s).
10. Discuss special features as needed.

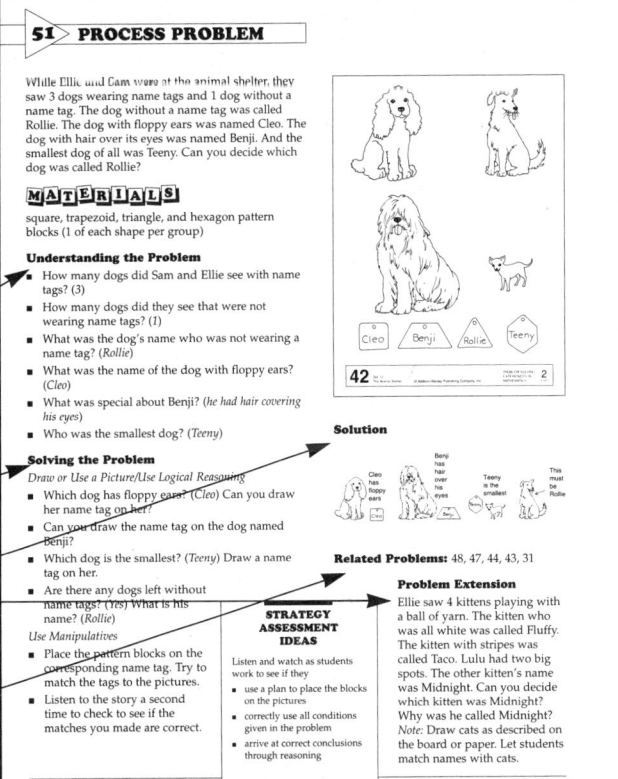

We have found this strategy (i.e., the ten teaching actions) to be a valuable and easily learned plan for facilitating students' thinking and problem-solving work. A scenario is useful to illustrate how to use the teaching actions.

Before students start work on a problem, have a whole-class discussion about the problem, following Teaching Actions 1, 2, and 3. After this discussion, have students begin working on the problem. **During** the time they are working on the problem, move around the room monitoring and directing students' work (Teaching Actions 4, 5, 6, and 7). Near the end of the time students are working on the problem, have two or three students place their solutions on the board. **After** they have solved the problem, have another whole-class discussion about the students' work (Teaching Actions 8, 9, and 10).

One of the key elements in successfully guiding students' problem-solving experiences is asking the right questions at the right time. For each problem, questions and hints are given in the lesson plan. The first set of questions (*Understanding the Problem*) should be used **before** students start work when you are helping them understand the problem (Teaching Action 2). The second set of questions (*Solving the Problem*) should be used **during** the time students are working on a problem, if or when they get stumped in their solution attempt (Teaching Action 5). The hints given for Solving the Problem should be viewed as *possible* hints.

Teaching Actions	Purpose of Teaching Action
BEFORE	
1. Read the problem to the class. Discuss words or phrases students may not understand.	To illustrate the importance of reading problems carefully and to focus on words that have special interpretations in mathematics.
2. Use a whole-class discussion about understanding the problem. Ask questions to help students understand the problem. (See the problem-specific hints for *Understanding the Problem*.)	To focus attention on important data in the problem and to clarify parts of the problem.
3. Ask students which strategies might be helpful for finding a solution. Do not evaluate students' suggestions. You can direct students' attention to the list of strategies on the problem-solving guide when asking for suggestions. (See page xiv.)	To elicit ideas for *possible* ways to solve a problem.
DURING	
4. Observe and question students about their work.	To diagnose students' strengths and weaknesses related to problem solving.
5. Give hints for solving the problem as needed. (See the problem-specific hints for *Solving the Problem*.)	To help students get past blocks in solving a problem.
6. Require students who obtain a solution to check their work and answer the problem.	To require students to look over their work.
7. Give a problem extension to students who complete the original problem much sooner than others. (See the *Problem Extension* section.)	To keep all students involved in a meaningful problem-solving experience until others have completed work on the original problem. (This is a classroom management teaching action. See Teaching Action 9 for using problem extensions to improve problem-solving ability.)
AFTER	
8. Show and discuss students' solutions to the original problem. Have students name the strategies used. You can reinforce the names of the strategies by pointing out the strategy names on the problem-solving guide. (See page xiv.)	To show and name strategies for solving the problem.
9. Relate the problem to previous problems (if possible) and solve an extension of the original problem. (See the *Related Problems* and *Problem Extension* sections.)	To demonstrate that problem-solving strategies are not problem-specific and to help students recognize different kinds of situations in which particular strategies may be useful.
10. Discuss special features of the original problem, if any. (See *Notes*.)	To show how special features of problems (for example, picture accompanying the problem statement) may influence students' thinking.

As you observe and question students, you must decide which, if any, of those hints are appropriate. Sometimes none of the hints listed will seem appropriate, and you will need to come up with others. Quite often you'll find it necessary to repeat one or more of the *Understanding the Problem* questions you used in the whole-class discussion **before** students started work. Most teachers find that selecting just the right hint for a student or group is a teaching skill that develops with experience.

In the *Solution* section, at least one solution to the problem is shown. The names of the solution strategies are given, and the answer to the problem is given in a complete sentence. The solutions shown for each problem were selected because they are ones used most often by students in our work with these problems. However, it is possible that students will use solution strategies different from the ones shown. That's fine! *Students should not be required to use a particular solution strategy for a given problem. Rather, they should be encouraged to find as many ways as possible to solve problems.*

The *Related Problems* section identifies (by number) problems that appeared earlier in the book that can be solved in ways similar to the given problem. The *Problem Extension* section includes an additional problem that is similar to the original problem. The answer to the problem extension is provided after the problem statement. Some problems have a *Comment* section containing an observation about the problems that could be used with Teaching Action 10 (discuss any special features of the problem). For example, some pictures accompanying problem statements can be misleading, and a statement to this effect could appear in this section.

TIME NEEDED TO IMPLEMENT THE PROGRAM This chart shows the amount of time you might expect to spend on the introductory stories and on each type of problem-solving experience if you use the complete set of teaching notes. It is important to realize that the time needed for each experience will be greatest at the beginning of the year. This is particularly true if your students have not had prior experience in a problem-solving program.

Type of experience	*Approximate time required*
introductory story	10 to 15 minutes
readiness and skill activity	5 to 10 minutes
process problem	15 to 20 minutes
one-step problem	5 to 10 minutes

One of the key elements in successfully guiding students' problem-solving experiences is asking the right questions at the right time.

Cooperative Learning for Problem Solving

The introductory stories should be handled as a whole-class discussion. We recommend that students work individually on readiness activities, skill activities, and one-step problems. For process problems, we recommend small-group work. Since process problems are usually challenging, small-group work helps reduce the pressure on the individual student, and it provides a structure for more easily monitoring and assessing the problem-solving performance of all the students in the class. Third, small-group work often elicits behaviors, such as justifying and evaluating ideas, that promote the improvement of problem-solving performance.

One of the important aspects in building successful cooperative group work for problem solving is to establish a class set of guidelines for working in groups. Consider devoting one class session at the start of the school year to developing a class set of guidelines. Invite students, working in groups, to list what they believe should be appropriate guidelines. Then, as a whole class, agree on a final list. Make a bulletin board displaying the guidelines, and refer to them on a regular basis before and after group work. Try not to have too many rules. Here are some guidelines students have suggested.

POSSIBLE SMALL-GROUP RULES
- Include everybody in the group.
- Share ideas.
- Talk only to your group.
- Participate.
- Cooperate with others.
- Pay attention.
- Be polite and kind to others.
- Listen.
- Follow directions.
- Talk quietly.
- Disagree when appropriate.
- Ask group questions only.

Using Manipulatives

Building and using models for important mathematical ideas helps most people to understand mathematics better. Models in the early grades are primarily *manipulative materials*. Manipulatives play a key role in every experience in this program at the kindergarten level and in many experiences at grades 1 and 2.

Suggested materials and tips for their use are provided in the lesson plans. The following manipulatives and other materials are called for in this book:

two-color counters (*optional*)
interlocking cubes
color counters
attribute blocks (*optional*)
pattern blocks
number tiles (*optional*)
cubes
play money
play pennies
popcorn kernels (*optional*)
crayons or markers

In many cases, alternative manipulatives can be used. For example, round 1" counters are commercially available, but other materials—such as 1" construction-paper squares, square tiles, buttons, or any other small counting objects—can be substituted for counters, depending on the activity. Two-color counters are commercially available, but pinto beans painted on one side and construction-paper squares marked on one side will work as well. An alternative for number tiles is paper squares numbered 1–12. Attribute blocks can be substituted for with other objects in the shapes of circles, triangles, squares, and nonsquare rectangles, such as attribute blocks, pattern blocks, counters, and paper shapes. The key to selecting a manipulative is its intended function in the problem.

Using manipulatives to solve problems may need to be modeled by you or other students to help all understand how the objects can be used to model mathematical situations.

Assessing Students

We have found three types of assessment tools particularly helpful in an assessment plan for problem solving: observations of student work, analyses of written work, and problem-solving portfolios.

An assessment plan for this program should not be limited to a check for correct answers.

OBSERVING AND LISTENING TO STUDENTS Every assessment plan for problem solving must be built on the observations you make as you watch and listen to students as they work. PSEM provides three kinds of support in this area. First, every process problem provides *Strategy Assessment Ideas*, actions and statements related to the implementation of problem-solving strategies to watch and listen for as students solve problems. Second, a *Strategy Implementation Checklist* is provided in the Assessment Appendix (see page 179). This list can be used to record students' progress over time in their ability to appropriately use strategies. Third, a general *Problem-Solving Observation Checklist*, also in the Assessment Appendix, includes general problem-solving behaviors and dispositions to be observed and analyzed over time.

ANALYZING WRITTEN WORK An alternative to observing and listening to students as they solve problems is to use a holistic system for assessing written work, including students' written solutions to problems and, possibly, their written explanations of their problem-solving processes. The Assessment Appendix includes a five-level *Focused Holistic Assessment Rubric*.

USING PORTFOLIOS A portfolio is a collection of student work. Portfolios can be used for many purposes, with the intended purpose determining the contents. A common use of portfolios is to provide a collection of student work that can be analyzed for growth over time. The work may be chosen by the student, by the teacher, or by both. Some possible kinds of work to include in portfolios are solutions to open-ended problems, a report of a group project, a mathematical autobiography, teacher-completed checklists, notes from an interview or observation, and a letter from the student to the reader of the portfolio. The Assessment Appendix includes a *Mathematics Portfolio Profile Checklist* for analyzing a student's portfolio for growth over time.

Here are some important things to keep in mind as you build your assessment plan for problem solving.

1. Assessment is not synonymous with grading.
2. An assessment plan should provide data useful in making instructional decisions.
3. All assessment plans should include observations and questioning of students.
4. Assessment should not be based on a single experience, but should look at student growth over time in a variety of kinds of experiences.
5. Every student does not have to be assessed in every problem-solving experience.

6. Assess thinking processes as well as the correct answer.
7. Assess attitudes and beliefs as well as performance.
8. Inform your students of your assessment plan.

Some Special Considerations

VALUE OF THE INTRODUCTORY STORIES Since students are not asked to solve mathematics problems in the discussions of the introductory stories, it is possible to underestimate the value of these stories. At the early grades, the context of the story is a problem characteristic that significantly affects students' abilities to understand problems. Although we have found the themes in this book to be interesting and familiar to most children, omitting an introductory story could influence their opportunity for success on the problem-solving experiences in that set.

REORGANIZING THE PROBLEM-SOLVING EXPERIENCES Should you decide to use only some of the problem-solving experiences in this book, the organization of the experiences has implications for how you should select and use them. *Do not start in the middle of the book.* The problem-solving experiences have been sequenced from easy to difficult. Even if you do not start the program near the beginning of the year, you should still begin with the first problem-solving experience in the book and move sequentially through the program.

A PROBLEM-SOLVING GUIDE Many teachers find the problem-solving guide shown below to be a helpful instructional aid in implementing the teaching actions for one-step and process problems. Most teachers make a bulletin board out of the guide, while some reproduce copies of the guide for individual students. The guide is particularly helpful for implementing Teaching Actions 3 and 8. For Teaching Actions 3 and 8, students use the guide when suggesting strategies that might be helpful in solving a given problem (Teaching Action 3) and in naming strategies actually used to solve problems (Teaching Action 8).

PROBLEM-SOLVING GUIDE

   Guess and Check
   Draw a Picture
   Use Addition
   Use Subtraction
   Make an Organized List
   Make a Table
   Look for a Pattern
   Use Logical Reasoning
   Use Objects

DEVELOP AN ASSESSMENT PLAN THAT IS COMPLETE YET EASY TO USE No one assessment technique can capture all aspects of students' thinking related to problem solving. So, build an assessment plan that looks at student work in several ways (e.g., observations, portfolios, written work), but be careful that your plan is reasonable to implement in the time available. It is better to use two or three assessment techniques well than several techniques poorly.

SET 1

Fire Station Number 1

Carrie's school bus drives by Fire Station Number 1 every day. Carrie always waves to the fire fighters if they're outside, and they always wave back. Even though all the children in the bus wave at the fire fighters, Carrie sometimes thinks the fire fighters are waving just at her!

One Monday morning, after Carrie's teacher collected lunch tickets, he told the class they were going on a field trip Friday to Fire Station Number 1. All of the children were excited, but especially Carrie, because she felt she already knew a lot of the fire fighters and they already knew her. The rest of the week, when Carrie rode by the fire station in the bus, she waved extra hard and extra long and yelled, "I'll see you Friday," even though she knew the fire fighters could not hear her.

When Carrie's bus arrived at the fire station on Friday morning, Carrie was the first one off the bus (after the teacher, of course). The first fire fighter Carrie saw said, "I know you! You wave to me almost every day and I wave back. I like it when you wave to me!" Carrie smiled and smiled and felt very happy. She was sure the fire fighters were already her friends.

Discussion Questions

1. Carrie waved to some special people on her way to school in the bus. Who were they? (*fire fighters*)
2. Were the fire fighters always outside to wave at Carrie? (*no*)
3. Why might the fire fighters not always be outside to wave at Carrie?
4. On which day was Carrie's field trip? (*Friday*)
5. Do you think the fire fighter knew Carrie's name? (*no*)
6. Have you ever visited a fire station? What did you see?

1 ▷ READINESS ACTIVITY

Answer Questions About a Story

Story A

The fire fighters keep a lot of pets at the fire station. They have 3 dogs (1 of them is a Dalmatian) and 2 cats. They also have 4 parakeets in a large cage.

Questions for Story A

1. What do the fire fighters keep at the fire station? (*pets*)
2. What kinds of pets do they have? (*dogs, cats, parakeets*)
3. What is one kind of dog they have? (*Dalmatian*)

Story B

Seven fire fighters sleep at the fire station every night in case there is a fire. If the alarm rings, 4 of them slide down a pole to get to the fire truck, and 3 run down the stairs.

Questions for Story B

1. How many fire fighters sleep at the station every night? (*7*)
2. Why do they sleep at the fire station? (*they can leave immediately from the station if there is a fire*)
3. How many fire fighters slide down a pole to get to the fire truck? (*4*)

TEACHING ACTIONS

1. Read Story A.
2. Ask questions for Story A.
3. Repeat for Story B.

2 ▷ READINESS ACTIVITY

Tell a Number Story

Story
There are buckets, ladders, nozzles, and hoses on the side of the fire trucks. A fire fighter said that one of the trucks has 7 ladders on it.

Task 1
Tell a story about something you might see at the fire station. Use the number 5 in your story.

Task 2
Tell a story about something you might see at a fire station, this time using the number 8 in your story.

TEACHING ACTIONS

1. Read and discuss the story.
2. Give Task 1 to the students. Encourage students to make up challenging stories. Solicit a variety of stories.
3. Repeat for Task 2.

3 PROCESS PROBLEM

Each fire fighter has 2 coats to wear. One coat is red and one is yellow. Each fire fighter also has 2 pairs of boots. One pair is red and one pair is yellow. How many ways can a fire fighter wear one of the coats and one of the pairs of boots?

MATERIALS

2-color counters, or red and yellow counters (or any 2 colors; at least 4 of each per group)

Understanding the Problem

- How many coats does each fire fighter have? (*2*) What colors are they? (*red and yellow*) Color the coats at the top of your paper.
- How many pairs of boots does each fire fighter have? (*2*) What colors are they? (*red and yellow*) Color the boots at the top of your paper.
- Why do fire fighters wear coats and boots to fires?
- Can a fire fighter wear a coat of one color and boots of a different color? (*yes*) Would a fire fighter wear one yellow boot and one red boot? (*probably not*)
- How many different ways can a fire fighter wear one of the coats and one of the pairs of boots? (*4*)

Solving the Problem

- If a fire fighter wears a yellow coat, what color boots can he or she wear? (*yellow or red*) What other color boots could the fire fighter wear? (*whichever was not named first*) Can you show this one way to dress by coloring your pictures?
- Pick one color coat. What color did you pick? Pick one color boots. What color did you pick?
- Color the top two coats yellow. What colors can you make the boots? (*red and yellow*) Color your pictures.

Use Manipulatives

- Use counters to show a red coat and red boots. Color your paper to show a red coat and red boots.
- If you turn over only *one* counter, what color coat and boots do you have now? Color your paper to show them.

- If you turn over *both* counters, what color coat and boots do you have now? Color your paper to show them.
- How many ways have you colored? (*4*)

Solution

Complete an Organized List

yellow coat   yellow coat
red boots   yellow boots

red coat   red coat
red boots   yellow boots

Problem Extension

Suppose each fire fighter also had an orange coat. Now how many different ways can each fire fighter wear a coat and boots? (*2 more ways or 6 in all*)

STRATEGY ASSESSMENT IDEAS

Listen and watch as students work to see if they

- create correct entries for their lists
- organize entries in their lists
- list all possibilities
- use manipulatives appropriately

4 ▸ PROCESS PROBLEM

A fire fighter can carry 2 full buckets of water at the same time. The fire fighters at Fire Station 1 have two different color buckets they use: one kind of bucket is red and one kind of bucket is yellow. The fire chief said there are 4 different ways to pick up 2 buckets. Can you find the 4 ways?

MATERIALS

2-color counters, or red and yellow counters (or any 2 colors; at least 4 of each per group)

Understanding the Problem

- How many buckets can a fire fighter carry at the same time? (*2*)
- Why would the fire fighter carry a bucket of water?
- What colors are the buckets? (*red and yellow*)
- How many different ways can a fire fighter pick up 2 of the colored buckets? (*4*)

Solving the Problem

Make an Organized List

- Could the fire fighter have one color bucket in one hand and a different color bucket in the other hand? (*yes*) Are there 2 ways to show this? (*yes*)
- Can you find and color the other 2 ways the fire fighter can carry the buckets?

Use Manipulatives

- Use counters to show that one of the fire fighters has a red bucket in one hand. What color bucket could the fire fighter have in the other hand? (*red or yellow*) Can you show this with the counters? Can you now show this by coloring the paper?
- Place counters to show the 4 ways the fire fighter could carry the buckets. Then color your paper to show each way you find.

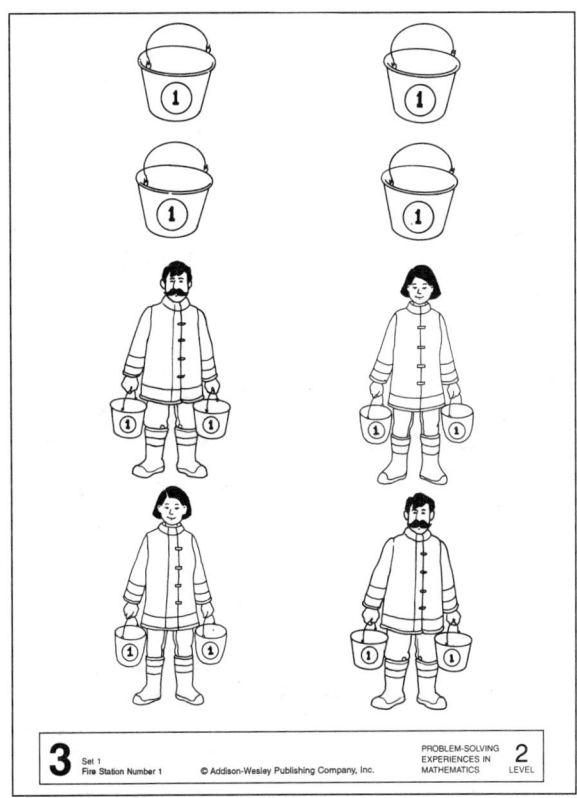

Related Problem: 3

Problem Extension

Suppose the buckets were black and red rather than yellow and red. Would there still be 4 different ways to carry 2 buckets? (*yes*) Can you tell the 4 ways?

Solution

red   red   yellow yellow

     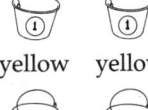
red   yellow   yellow red

STRATEGY ASSESSMENT IDEAS

Listen and watch as students work to see if they

- create correct entries for their lists
- organize entries in their lists
- list all possibilities
- use manipulatives appropriately

Insects in the Garden

Do you know what insects are? Wherever you live, there are insects all around you. We have all seen ants, beetles, bees, and butterflies. Insects live in parks and gardens, and some even live in people's homes. If you are quiet and patient, you may have a chance to watch some insects work or eat.

Insects do a lot of different things. During the spring and summer you may see a bee gathering pollen from a flower or see a butterfly resting on a branch of a tree. If you look carefully you may even see two ants meet on a path and touch antennas before scurrying off about their business.

Ants are very hard workers and they are very strong for their size. Many times ants carry things such as grains of dirt or bread crumbs that are as big or even bigger than they are. Usually when you see ants carrying dirt, they are digging in the ground to make a home and carrying the dirt away. When you see ants carrying bread crumbs or other small bits of food, they are carrying the food back to their home to share with the other ants.

The next time you go to the park or out into your own yard, look around you in the grass, bushes, and trees. If you look closely you will probably find some insects doing what insects do—working, gathering food, building homes, or just resting.

Discussion Questions

1. What are some kinds of insects? (*ants, beetles, bees, butterflies*)
2. Where can you find insects? (*parks, gardens, homes*)
3. What kinds of insects might you find in your house?
4. Why do bees gather pollen?
5. Have you ever seen a butterfly? Can you describe it?
6. Have you ever seen ants carrying things?
7. What other insects can you think of?

5 ▷ READINESS ACTIVITY

Answer Questions About a Story

Story A

Jerry and Beth went to the park to look for butterflies. Butterflies were harder to find than they thought they would be. By the end of the day, they had spotted 3 blue-and-yellow butterflies and 4 orange-and-white butterflies.

Questions for Story A

1. Why did Jerry and Beth go to the park? (*to look for butterflies*)
2. How many blue-and-yellow butterflies did they find? (*3*)
3. How many orange-and-white butterflies did they find? (*4*)
4. Why do you think butterflies might be hard to find?

Story B

Aisha watched one of the ants in an ant colony in her yard. First, she saw the ant carrying 2 grains of dirt at the same time. A few minutes later, she saw the ant carrying 3 grains of dirt. Aisha thought this ant was probably the strongest ant in the world.

Questions for Story B

1. Why did Aisha think the ant was so strong? (*it carried more than 1 grain of dirt at a time*)
2. What did the ant do that amazed Aisha? (*it carried 3 grains of dirt*)
3. Do you think the ant was the strongest ant in the world?
4. Have you sever seen an ant carrying grains of dirt?

TEACHING ACTIONS

1. Read Story A.
2. Ask the questions for Story A.
3. Repeat for Story B.

6 READINESS ACTIVITY

Tell a Number Story

Story

Josie went to her garden to pick some flowers. While she was in the garden, she saw 3 bees flying around the flowers. The bees were getting pollen from the flowers to make honey.

Task 1

Make up a number story about bees getting pollen from flowers. Use the number 4 in your story.

Task 2

Choose your own number and make up a story about bees and flowers that uses your number.

TEACHING ACTIONS

1. Read and discuss the story.
2. Give Task 1 to the students. Encourage students to make up interesting stories. Solicit several stories.
3. Repeat for Task 2.

7 ▶ PROCESS PROBLEM

Josie and two friends wanted to pick 11 different flowers. When they were picking flowers, each of them took all of the flowers from one of the flower pots. Which flower pots did the flowers come from?

MATERIALS

interlocking cubes in 5 colors (at least 11 of each color per group)

Understanding the Problem

- How many people picked flowers? (*3*)
- How many flowers did Josie and her friends want to pick? (*11*)
- What are we trying to find? (*which flower pots the flowers came from*)

Solving the Problem

Guess and Check

- Can you find 3 numbers that add up to 11?
- Are any of those combinations in the picture? (*see solution*)
- If Josie picked 2 flowers from a single pot, how many flowers will her two friends pick if they pick a total of 11? (*9*)

Use Manipulatives

- Have students place one cube on top of each flower. If possible, each pot of flowers should contain a single color of cubes.
- Each of the 3 students in a group will "pick flowers from one pot" by taking all the cubes from a flower pot on the activity sheet.
- The 3 students in the group each tell how many cubes they have. Then, students combine the 3 sets of cubes to see if they have 11, more than 11, or fewer than 11.

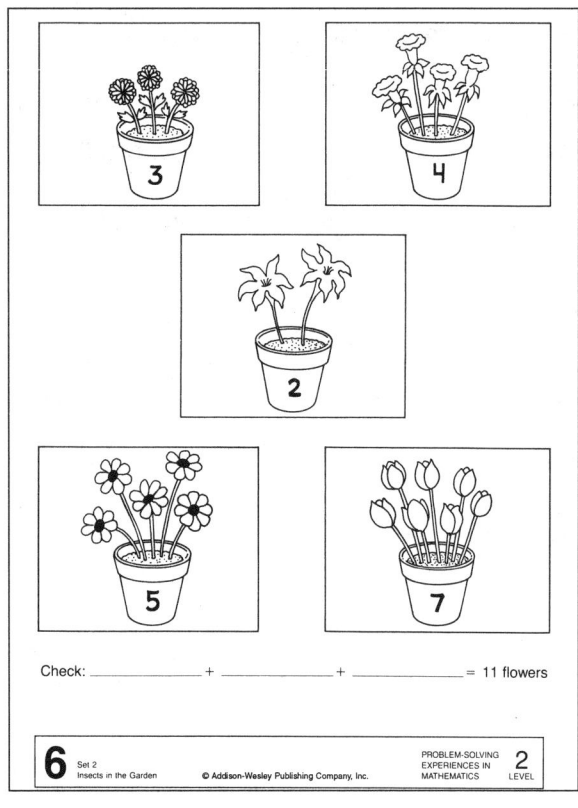

Solution

Guess and Check/Use Manipulatives

- Try 3 + 4 + 2 = 9 (*too low*)
- Try 3 + 4 + 5 = 12 (*too high*)
- Try 2 + 4 + 5 = 11 (*correct*)

The friends picked flowers from the pots with 2, 4, and 5 flowers in them.

Note: There are other ways to guess and check.

Related Problems: 4, 3

Problem Extension

Is it possible for the 3 children to pick a total of 12 flowers? (*yes: 7, 3, 2*)

STRATEGY ASSESSMENT IDEAS

Listen and watch as students work to see if they

- make a reasonable first guess (the guess should include numbers from 3 different pots)
- make a second guess using what they learn from checking with cubes
- can give good reasons for their guesses

8 > PROCESS PROBLEM

Tom and Sue counted the number of petals on 3 flowers. When they finished, they had counted 12 petals in all. Which flowers did they count the petals on?

Understanding the Problem

- What did Tom and Sue count? (*petals on flowers*)
- How many flowers did they use? (*3*)
- What is a petal? (*a part of a flower*)
- How many petals did they count on the 3 flowers? (*12*)
- Are we trying to find how many flowers they counted? (*no, which flowers they counted the petals on*)

Solving the Problem

- Can you find 3 numbers that add up to 12?
- Can you try 3 of the numbers in the picture and see if they add up to 12?
- If Tom and Sue counted a flower with 3 petals, how many more petals did they count? (*9*) Which flowers have those many petals? (*2 and 7 or 4 and 5*)
- Is there more than one solution to this problem? (*yes; 3 + 2 + 7 = 12 and 3 + 4 + 5 = 12*)

Solution

Guess and Check

- Try 3 + 2 + 4 = 9 (*too few*)
- Try 3 + 2 + 5 = 10 (*too few*)
- Try 3 + 2 + 7 = 12 (*correct*)

Tom and Sue counted the petals on the flowers with 3, 2, and 7 petals.

Note: Encourage students who find one solution to look for another, 3 + 4 + 5 = 12.

Related Problem: 7

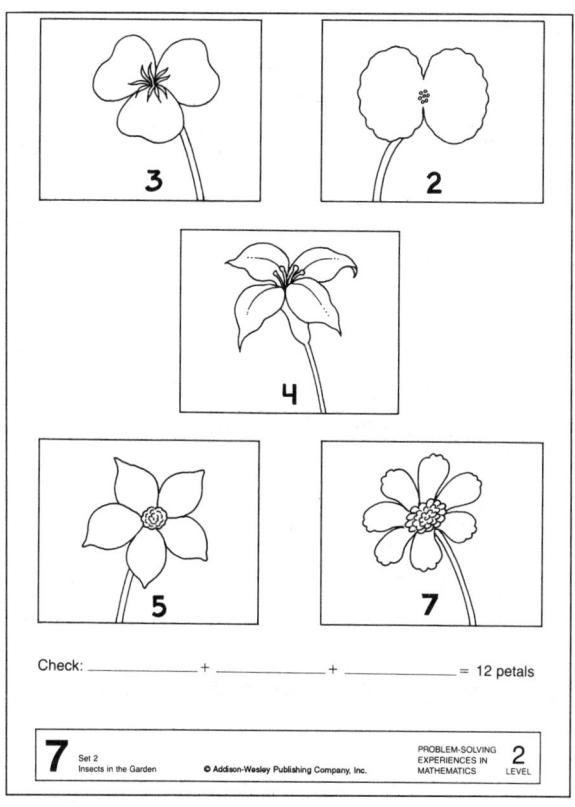

Problem Extension

Tom and Sue counted the number of petals on 3 flowers. When they finished, they had counted 9 petals in all. Two of the flowers had the same number of petals. How many petals did each flower have? (*there are 3 solutions: 1 + 1 + 7; 2 + 2 + 5; 4 + 4 + 1*)

STRATEGY ASSESSMENT IDEAS

Listen and watch as students work to see if they

- make a reasonable first guess (guess must include the number of petals on 3 flowers)
- make a second guess using what they learn from checking their first guess

SET 3

Butterflies and Flowers

Ana and David were walking in the park near their house one day when they saw a beautiful blue, black, and yellow butterfly. It fluttered down near them and lit on the branch of a small rose bush. The butterfly spread its wings open to the warm sun. Then it slowly raised its wings and brought them together above its back. Ana and David crept closer to have a better look. David carefully picked up the butterfly and put it on the back of his hand.

"Why, it's lighter than a feather," he whispered. When he spoke the butterfly suddenly spread its wings and flew to the top of a fence nearby.

Ana said, "Look, David, it left some powdery stuff on your hand—'butterfly dust'."

As the children continued on their walk, they saw lots of animals: squirrels, birds, and even a small green frog, but no more butterflies.

The next day they went for another walk in the park. This time their cat, Cleo, went with them. They walked to a part of the park they had never seen before. In this part of the park there was a small field full of clover and dandelions. The best part was that there were more butterflies than they could count. Cleo got excited when she saw them and began to try to catch one. She jumped and jumped high above the clover but she never did catch one. If she had caught one, she would have eaten it because she liked butterflies as much as mice. Ana and David were happy that Cleo never caught one—they thought butterflies were just too beautiful to be eaten, even by their family cat.

Discussion Questions

1. What did David pick up during his walk in the park? (*a butterfly*)
2. What colors did the butterfly have? (*blue, black, yellow*)
3. What did the butterfly do when David whispered to Ana? (*flew away*)
4. What did the butterfly leave on David's hand? (*powdery "butterfly dust"*)
5. What other animals did Ana and David see? (*squirrels, birds, frog*)
6. Who went to the park with them the next day? (*their cat, Cleo*)
7. What was in the field they walked to? (*clover and dandelions*)
8. Were there many butterflies in the field? (*yes*)
9. What did Cleo try to do? (*catch the butterflies*)
10. Why were Ana and David glad that Cleo didn't catch a butterfly? (*they thought butterflies were too beautiful to be eaten*)

9 ▷ READINESS ACTIVITY

Visualize a Story

Story A

Imagine that you are walking in a park on a sunny day. In the park there are lots of colorful flowers and tall trees. Suddenly, a beautiful butterfly flies nearby and comes to rest on the branch of a small bush.

Story B

Suppose you have a cat named Cleo that likes to chase butterflies. One day you go to a park to look for butterflies. Both you and Cleo have a lot of fun chasing butterflies. When you catch one, you look closely at it as you hold it loosely in your hands. Then you let it go and it flies away.

TEACHING ACTIONS

1. Have students close their eyes.
2. Tell them to picture in their minds the story you will read to them.
3. Read Story A.
4. Ask students to describe what they visualized. Ask them to describe the park and the butterfly.
5. Repeat for Story B. Ask students to tell you what Cleo looks like and to describe the butterfly they catch.

10 ▷ READINESS ACTIVITY

Retell a Number Story

Story

Six butterflies were sunning themselves on top of a wooden fence. After a while, four of the butterflies flew away.

Task 1

Retell the story with a different number of butterflies.

Task 2

Retell the story with birds sitting in a tree instead of butterflies on a fence.

TEACHING ACTIONS

1. Read and discuss the story.
2. Give Task 1 to the students.
3. Solicit stories with different numbers of butterflies in them.
4. Give Task 2 to the students.
5. Solicit stories from several students to get variety.

11 > PROCESS PROBLEM

David decided to make a butterfly poster for a school project. He drew pictures of only the most beautiful butterflies he had seen. He arranged his drawings of butterflies in nice, neat rows. Each row made a pattern. Can you decide which butterflies David will put in his collection next? n. Can you decide which butterflies David will put in his collection next?

MATERIALS

crayons or markers in appropriate colors (at least blue, red, and yellow)

Understanding the Problem
- Why did David make a butterfly poster? (*for a school project*)
- What is a butterfly poster?
- How did he arrange his butterfly drawings? (*in neat rows in a pattern*)
- What do we want to find out about David's butterfly poster? (*which butterflies go in spots 1 and 2*)

Solving the Problem
- Have students color the butterflies as follows: first row—blue, red, yellow; second row—blue, red, yellow; third row—blue.
- What color is the middle butterfly in each row (point to them)? (*red*)
- How many dots on each wing does the middle butterfly in each row have (point to them)? (*1 dot on each wing*)
- Can you color the butterfly the color you think belongs in spot 1? (*see solution*)
- Can you look at the last butterfly in each row (point to them) and decide which butterfly goes in spot 2? (*see solution*)

Solution

Look for a Pattern

Pattern: blue, red, yellow; dots alternate 4, 2, 4

A red, 2-dot butterfly goes in spot 1, and a yellow, 4-dot butterfly goes in spot 2.

STRATEGY ASSESSMENT IDEAS

Listen and watch as students work to see if they
- describe a pattern formed by the arrangement of butterflies
- extend the pattern correctly
- use the pattern to arrive at the correct answer

Problem Extension

One day David rearranged his butterfly poster into a different pattern. Can you tell which 2 butterflies are missing?

Note: The color pattern might be R, R, R and B, B, B and Y, Y, Y. Both of the missing butterflies are yellow with 4 dots.

16

12 PROCESS PROBLEM

Ana and David planted large and small flowers in their garden. Some flowers had 3 petals and some had 5 petals. The flowers were planted in a pattern. Two flowers have not bloomed yet. When they bloom, what will they look like? To find out, finish the pattern of flowers.

Understanding the Problem

- What sizes of flowers did Ana and David plant? (*large and small*)
- Did all the flowers have the same number of petals? (*no, some had 3 and some had 5*)
- How many flowers have not bloomed yet? (*2*)
- What are we trying to find? (*what the 2 flowers will look like*)

Solving the Problem

- How is flower 2 different from flower 1? (*it is smaller*)
- How is flower 3 different from flower 2? (*it is larger and has only 3 petals*)
- Can you tell how each flower is different from the one just before it? Can you see a pattern? (*see solution*)
- The pattern begins: large, small, large, small, large, small. What will come next? (*large, small*)
- The number of petals follows the pattern: 5, 5, 3, 3, 5, 5. What will come next? (*3, 3*)
- Have students write the numeral 7 under the first flower that comes next and 8 under the second one.

Solution

Look for a Pattern

Pattern: large 5-petal, small 5-petal, large 3-petal, small 3-petal, and so on

The next 2 flowers are large 3-petal, small 3-petal.

Related Problem: 11

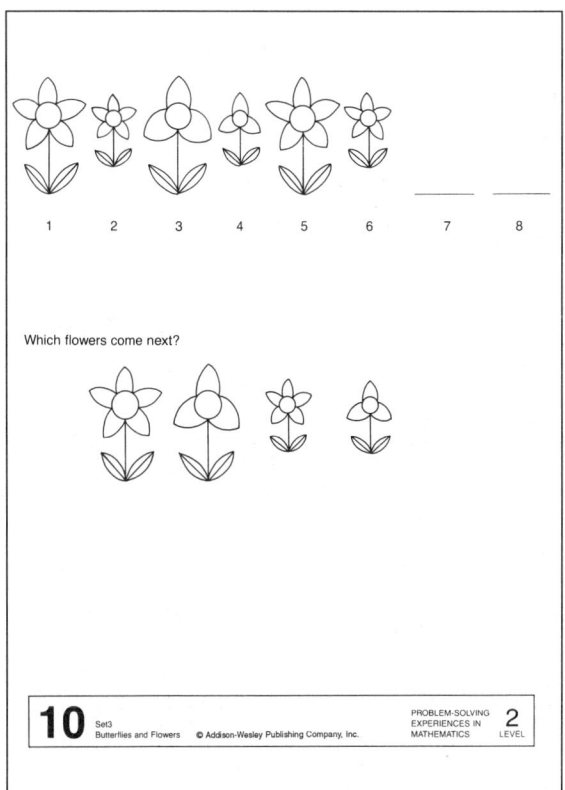

Problem Extension

Ana and David planted a different number of flower seeds each day for 7 days. The table shows how many seeds they planted on the first 4 days. (Copy the table onto the board.) Do you see a pattern? How many seeds did they plant on the other days? (*9, 11, 13*)

Day 1	Day 2	Day 3	Day 4	Day 5	Day 6	Day 7
1	3	5	7			

STRATEGY ASSESSMENT IDEAS

Listen and watch as students work to see if they

- describe a pattern formed by the arrangement of flowers
- extend the pattern correctly
- use the pattern to arrive at the correct answer

The Oakdale Earth Savers

At Oakdale School one day, all the teachers and children went to the gym for a special program about taking care of the environment and recycling. The children learned about many things that can be recycled and used again. They talked about how trees are used to make paper, and how used paper can be used to make newspaper and other kinds of paper products. They learned about different kinds of plastic, like soft plastic and hard plastic. They learned about different kinds of glass, like green glass and clear glass. They talked about what happens to a piece of garbage after it is thrown in a trash can.

After the program, many children in the school were interested in recycling and learning more about how to help take care of the environment. They wanted to do something to help the environment.

Ms. Sanchez started a club for these children. They called their club the Earth Savers Club. Twenty-four students came to the first meeting of the Earth Savers Club.

Discussion Questions

1. Where did the teachers and children at Oakdale School go one day? (*to the gym*)
2. Why did they go to the gym? (*for a special program about taking care of the environment*)
3. What were many of the students interested in after the program? (*recycling and taking care of the environment*)
4. Who started a club for these students? (*Ms. Sanchez*)
5. What was the club called? (*Earth Savers Club*)
6. How many students attended the first meeting? (*24*)

13 ▷ READINESS ACTIVITY

Visualize a Story

Story A
Ms. Sanchez said that the Earth Savers Club could fix up a corner of a classroom for their program. They put recycling bins in the corner and pictures of the Earth all over the walls.

Story B
The club members decided to make a membership card they could carry and show to other members. They each made their own card, but they all drew the same picture to show they were in the Earth Savers Club.

TEACHING ACTIONS

1. Have students close their eyes.
2. Tell students to picture in their minds the story you will read.
3. Read Story A.
4. Ask students to describe what they visualized.
5. Repeat for Story B.

14 ▷ READINESS ACTIVITY

Retell a Number Story

Story A
The Earth Savers Club has 4 barrels to collect recyclable paper. They also have 6 bins to put recyclable glass in.

Story B
Dennis, Pedro, and Debbie decided that to be in the Earth Savers Club you had to be at least 6 years old, but you could not be more than 9 years old.

TEACHING ACTIONS

1. Read and discuss Story A.
2. Have students retell Story A using different numbers. Solicit a variety of stories.
3. Repeat for Story B.

15 ▶ PROCESS PROBLEM

When families arrived to pick up the children after the Earth Saver Club's first meeting, Ms. Sanchez showed them buttons she could order for the club members to wear. Each button costs $3. Maria's mother said she would pay for 5 of the buttons. How much did Maria's mother pay for the 5 buttons? Complete the table to help you find out.

MATERIALS

counters (10 per pair); play money (at least $15 per pair)

Understanding the Problem

- What did Ms. Sanchez want to order for the club members? (*buttons*) How much did each one of the buttons cost? (*$3*)
- Did Maria buy buttons for the club? (*no, her mother did*)
- What do we want to find? (*how much 5 buttons cost*)

Solving the Problem

Complete a Table/Look for a Pattern

- What numbers are given in the top row of the table? (*1–5*) What do these number show? (*number of buttons*) What do the numbers in the bottom row show? (*cost of buttons*)
- If one button costs $3, how much does it cost to buy 2 buttons? (*$6*) Can you find a way to see how much it would cost for all 5 buttons?

Use Manipulatives

- How can you place the counters to show how much 1 button would cost? Two buttons? Do you see a pattern? Can you tell how much 5 buttons would cost by completing the pattern?

STRATEGY ASSESSMENT IDEAS

Listen and watch as students work to see if they

- place numbers correctly in the table
- use a pattern to correctly extend the table
- interpret the table to arrive at the correct answer

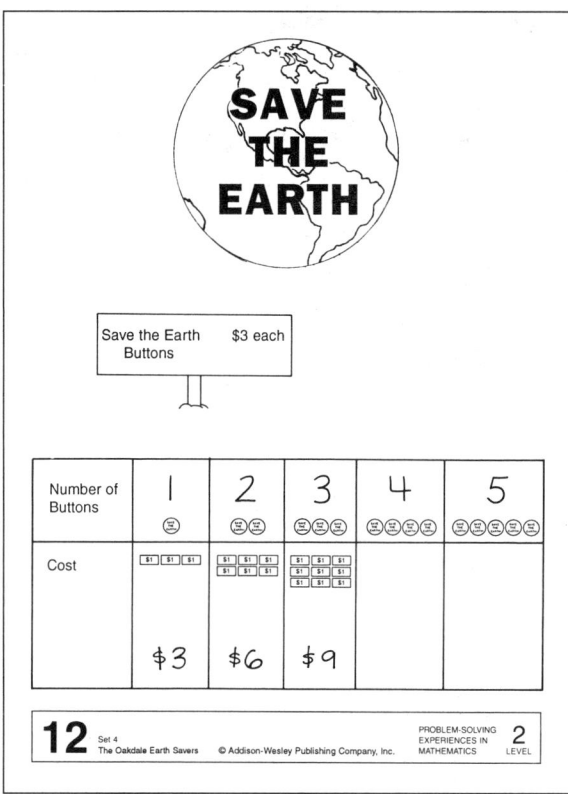

Solution

Number of Buttons	1	2	3	4	5
Cost	$3	$6	$9	$12	$15

5 buttons cost $15.

Related Problems: 12, 11

Problem Extension

How much would it cost to buy 12 buttons? (*$36*)

16 PROCESS PROBLEM

At each meeting the Earth Savers Club planned projects. Their projects helped to clean up their school and community. At one meeting the club decided to start saving aluminum cans. For every 3 cans the children collected, the recycling company would give them 2¢. The next week, club members brought a total of 18 cans to their meeting, but they were having trouble figuring out how much money they would get when they took the cans to be recycled. Complete the table to find how much would they get for the cans they collected.

MATERIALS

counters (at least 18 per group); pennies (at least 12 per group)

Understanding the Problem

- What did the club members collect? (*aluminum cans*)
- What did they plan to do with their cans? (*sell them to the recycling company*)
- How many cans did they collect? (*18*)

Solving the Problem

Complete a Table/Look for a Pattern

- Look at the table. How much money did the club get for 3 cans? (*2¢*) For 6 cans? (*4¢*) For 9 cans? (*6¢*)
- Look at the bottom row. Do you see a pattern in the numbers? What number should go in the first empty space? (*10¢*) The next empty space? (*12¢*)

Use Manipulatives

- Students use counters to represent the cans. Match up 3 counters with 2 pennies. Place a group of 3 counters and 2 pennies in each section of the table.
- Label the first squares with 3 cans and 2¢.
- Move the material from the first section of the table and combine it with the second section. If the students had 6 cans, how much money would they make? (*4¢*)
- Continue combining manipulatives and labeling the table.
- Use the table to find how much money the children will make.

STRATEGY ASSESSMENT IDEAS

Listen and watch as students work to see if they

- place counters and pennies correctly in the table
- use a pattern to correctly extend the table
- interpret the table to arrive at the correct answer

Solution

Number of Cans	3	6	9	12	15	18
Cost	2¢	4¢	6¢	8¢	10¢	12¢

The club got 12¢ for 18 cans.

Related Problems: 15, 12, 11

Problem Extension

The children decided to use their profit to buy garbage bags for use in picking up trash. They can buy garbage bags for 3¢ each. How many bags can they buy with the money they made from their 18 cans? Use manipulatives to show your answer. (*3 garbage bags*)

SET 5

Guinea Pig Pets

Emmy and Holly's teacher brought two guinea pigs to school one day for the children to play with. After that, Emmy and Holly just knew they wanted guinea pigs of their own. Emmy and Holly asked their parents if they could have guinea pigs for pets, and their parents said yes.

Emmy and Holly each got three guinea pigs. Emmy named hers Zorro, Speedy, and Hopalong. Zorro is all black. Speedy and Hopalong are brown and white. Holly named her guinea pigs Ernie, Bingo, and Kermit. All of Holly's guinea pigs are brown and white.

On Saturdays, Emmy and Holly get together and let their guinea pigs play. The guinea pigs like to play together, but Emmy and Holly really have the most fun. Holly scratches her guinea pigs under their chins and they seem to like it. Emmy tried scratching under her guinea pigs' chins but they would scamper away.

Every night, Emmy and Holly place a blanket over the guinea pigs' cages just after they say goodnight to them. They take good care of their new guinea pigs.

Discussion Questions

1. What did Emmy and Holly ask their parents if they could have for pets? (*guinea pigs*)
2. How did they get the idea they wanted guinea pigs? (*the teacher brought two to school one day for the children to play with*)
3. How many guinea pigs did each girl get? (*3*)
4. Do you remember any of the guinea pigs' names? (*Zorro, Speedy, Hopalong, Ernie, Bingo, Kermit*)
5. Were all the guinea pigs the same color? (*no*)
6. What do Emmy and Holly do for their guinea pigs at night? (*place a blanket over the cages*)
7. If you had three guinea pigs, what would you name them?

17 ▶ SKILL ACTIVITY

Tell a Question

Story A
The Town & Country Pet Shop has 4 brown-and-white guinea pigs for sale and 5 black guinea pigs for sale.

Possible Questions for Story A
1. How many guinea pigs are for sale altogether? (9)
2. How many more black guinea pigs than brown-and-white guinea pigs are for sale? (1)

Story B
Emmy's father had 7 guinea pigs when he was 8 years old. Emmy is 8 years old and has 3 guinea pigs.

Possible Question for Story B
How many more guinea pigs did Emmy's father have than Emmy has? (4)

TEACHING ACTIONS
1. Read Story A to the students.
2. Have students tell questions they can answer using data from the story. Solicit a variety of questions.
3. (optional) Have students find the answers to the questions.
4. Repeat for Story B.

18 ONE-STEP PROBLEM

Emmy wanted to buy two cage liners for her guinea pig cage. She bought a large cage liner and a small cage liner. The large ones were on sale for 8¢ each and the small ones were on sale for 5¢ each. How much did it cost to buy the two cage liners?

MATERIALS

pennies or counters (optional; at least 15 per group)

Understanding the Problem

- What did Emmy want to buy for her guinea pigs' cage? (*cage liners*)
- How many cage liners did she buy? (*2*)
- Were the ones she bought the same size? (*no*)
- Did the two cage liners cost the same amount? (*no*) How much did each cost? (*8¢ and 5¢*)
- Why do you think she only bought two cage liners when she has three guinea pigs?
- What are we trying to find? (*how much the 2 cage liners will cost*)

Solving the Problem

- If one cage liner cost 1¢ and another 2¢, what would it cost to buy both? (*3¢*) Which operation did you use? (*addition*)
- Are you trying to find how much more the large cage liner cost? (*no*)
- To find the total, which operation should you use? (*addition*)
- Can you use pennies to help you solve this problem?

Solution

Choose the Operation

8¢ + 5¢ = 13¢   or   8¢
                       + 5¢
                       ―――
                        13¢

The 2 cage liners cost 13¢.

Problem Extensions

1. How much more does a large cage liner cost than a small cage liner? (*8¢ − 5¢ = 3¢ more*)
2. Suppose Emmy bought two large cage liners. What would the cost be? (*8¢ + 8¢ = 16¢*)

19 PROCESS PROBLEM

Emmy's 3 guinea pigs, Zorro, Speedy, and Hopalong, were all different sizes. Zorro was the smallest. Hopalong was bigger than Speedy. Can you match each guinea pig with its name tag?

Understanding the Problem

- How many guinea pigs does Emmy have? (*3*)
- What are the guinea pigs' names? (*Zorro, Speedy, and Hopalong*)
- Are the guinea pigs all the same? (*no, they are different sizes*)
- What do you know about Zorro? (*Zorro is the smallest*)
- Is Hopalong bigger or smaller than Speedy? (*bigger*)

Solving the Problem

- Can you find the picture of the smallest guinea pig? (*see solution*) Which guinea pig is this? (*Zorro*) Draw a line from Zorro's name tag to the picture of the smallest guinea pig.
- If Hopalong is bigger than Speedy, which of the remaining two guinea pigs must be Hopalong? (*see solution*)

Solution

Use a Picture/Use Logical Reasoning

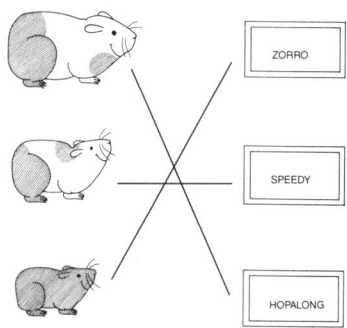

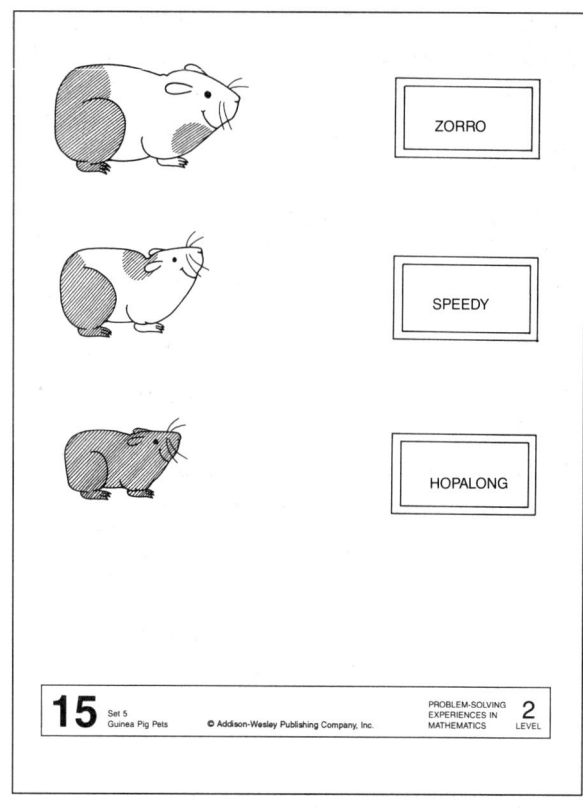

Related Problem: 7

Problem Extensions

1. Suppose Zorro were the largest guinea pig, not the smallest. Which guinea pig would be the smallest? (*Speedy*)
2. Suppose Zorro were the middle-size guinea pig, not the smallest or largest. Which guinea pig would be the smallest? (*Speedy*)

STRATEGY ASSESSMENT IDEAS

Listen and watch as students work to see if they

- use a plan to record their work on the picture
- correctly use all conditions given in the problem
- arrive at correct conclusions through reasoning

20 PROCESS PROBLEM

Holly likes to draw her guinea pigs and draw costumes on them. She draws a hat on one guinea pig, sunglasses on another guinea pig, a bow tie on the third guinea pigs. The guinea pigs' names are Bingo, Ernie, and Kermit. Holly draws a bow on Ernie. She does not draw sunglasses on Bingo. Can you match each guinea pig drawing with its name tag?

Understanding the Problem

- How many guinea pigs does Holly have? (*3*) What are their names? (*Bingo, Ernie, and Kermit*)
- What does she do with her guinea pigs? (*she draws them*)
- Does she draw them all wearing the same thing? (*no*)
- What does she put on her guinea pig drawings? (*hat, sunglasses, bow tie*)
- Holly draws a bow tie on which guinea pig? (*Ernie*)
- What does Holly not draw on Bingo? (*sunglasses*)

Solving the Problem

- Find the drawing of the guinea pig wearing a bow tie. Which guinea pig is this? (*Ernie*) Draw a line from Ernie to his name tag.
- If Holly does not draw Bingo with sunglasses, which guinea pig does she draw wearing the sunglasses? (*Kermit*)

Solution

Use a Picture/Use Logical Reasoning

Related Problems: 19, 7

Problem Extension

Suppose Holly draws a hat on Ernie. On which guinea pig would she draw sunglasses? (*Kermit*)

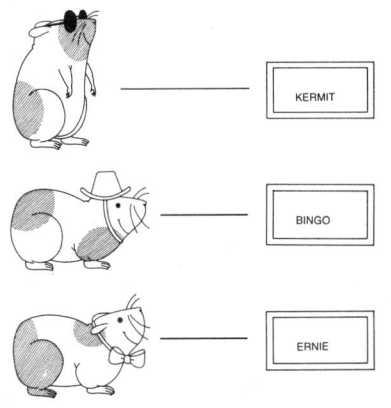

STRATEGY ASSESSMENT IDEAS

Listen and watch as students work to see if they

- use a plan to record their work on the picture
- correctly uses all conditions given in the problem
- arrive at correct conclusions through reasoning

The Scavenger Hunt

Ruth, Gloria, Mike, and Ron were bored! It was a hot summer afternoon and none of them could think of anything exciting to do. Can you imagine—four 7-year-olds with nothing to do? Ruth suggested that they play kickball, but Gloria and Mike said it was too hot outside to run. Then Ron had an idea: "Let's go for a swim and cool off." Everyone thought Ron had a good idea; everyone except Gloria, that is. Gloria couldn't go swimming because she had a broken arm (she fell roller blading). "I'm sorry," she said, "but I can't go swimming because I can't get my cast wet." They all agreed that if Gloria couldn't go swimming, none of them would go. They wanted Gloria to play with them.

"I have an idea," said Mike. "Let's ask my sister, Kate. She always has good ideas." Kate, who was 11 years old and knew lots of exciting things to do, was sitting in a swing reading a book. She said, "In this book I'm reading, the boys and girls went on a scavenger hunt. It sounded like a lot of fun to me. Do you want to learn about scavenger hunts?" Of course, they all did. Here is what a scavenger hunt is all about.

Ruth and Mike are on one team and Gloria and Ron are on another team. Each team writes down a list of used things that everyone knows about but that may be hard to find. The two teams exchange lists and then they go around their neighborhood and try to find the things on their lists. The team that finds the most things wins.

The boys and girls made up lists and off they went on the scavenger hunt. They had forgotten all about being bored.

Discussion Questions

1. Why were the boys and girls bored? (*they couldn't think of anything to do*)
2. Why did they decide not to play kickball? (*it was too hot to run*)
3. Why couldn't Gloria go swimming? (*she had a cast on her broken arm*)

4. Why did Ruth, Mike, and Ron decide not to go swimming? (*they wanted Gloria to play with them*)
5. How old was Mike's sister, Kate? (*11*)
6. What idea did Kate have? (*scavenger hunt*)
7. Where did Kate get her idea for a scavenger hunt? (*from a book she was reading*)
8. Have you ever been on a scavenger hunt?
9. Do you know what to do to get ready for a scavenger hunt?

21 READINESS ACTIVITY

Act Out a Story Situation

Story A

To prepare for the scavenger hunt, Ruth and Mike made a list of things to find. Gloria and Ron also made a list of things. Then they exchanged lists and began to hunt for the things on their lists.

Story B

Gloria and Ron had 9 things to find on their list. After hunting all day they found only 4 of the things on their list. They decided to stop looking and start again the next day.

Note (Story B): Have the director tell the students who are acting the roles of Gloria and Ron to write down 9 things on a sheet of paper. The 9 items should be things familiar to the students (for example, old tennis ball, broken shoe string, and pencil with an eraser).

TEACHING ACTIONS

1. Read and discuss Story A.
2. Have one student direct others to act out Story A.
3. Discuss what the students have acted out. Ask if it was the same as the story.
4. Repeat with Story B with a different student as director.

22 ONE-STEP PROBLEM

Ruth and Mike were a team and Gloria and Ron were another team for the scavenger hunt. Ruth and Mike had 7 things to find on their list and Gloria and Ron had 9 things to find on their list. How many things were there on the two lists?

Understanding the Problem

- What is a scavenger hunt?
- Who was on Ruth's team? (*Mike*)
- Who was on Ron's team? (*Gloria*)
- How many things did Ruth and Mike have to find? (*7*)
- How many things did Gloria and Ron have to find? (*9*)
- What are we trying to find? (*how many things were on the 2 lists*)

Solving the Problem

- Do you need to add or subtract to find the answer? (*add*)
- What numbers will you add? (*7 and 9*)
- Can you write a number sentence using the number of things on each list? (*7 + 9 = 16*)

Solution

Choose the Operation

7 + 9 = 16   or   7
                    + 9
                   ____
                    16

There were 16 things on the two lists.

Related Problem: 18

Problem Extension

Ruth and Mike had 7 things to find on their list and Gloria and Ron had 9 things to find on their list. How many more things did Gloria and Ron have to find than Ruth and Mike? (*9 – 7 = 2*)

23 ▸ PROCESS PROBLEM

After hunting for 1 hour, the children stopped to rest and look at what they had found. Each child had found one thing. They decided to try to figure out who had found each thing. Ruth said, "The thing I found used to be hit with a racquet." Gloria said, "What I found used to fly in the sky on a windy day." Ron said, "I found something that a person can write with but can't be used to correct writing mistakes." What did each of the four children find?

MATERIALS

pieces of scrap paper (on which to write the names of what was found)

Understanding the Problem

- How long did the children look before they stopped to rest? (*1 hour*)
- How many things had each child found? (*1*)
- What are we trying to find? (*what 1 thing each child found*)

Solving the Problem

- Can you write Ruth's name under what she found? (*tennis ball*)
- Gloria found something that used to fly on a windy day. What could that be? Write her name under that thing. (*kite*)
- What did Ron find? Write his name under what he found. (*pencil without eraser*)
- Can you figure out what Mike found? How do you know?

Solution

Use Logical Reasoning

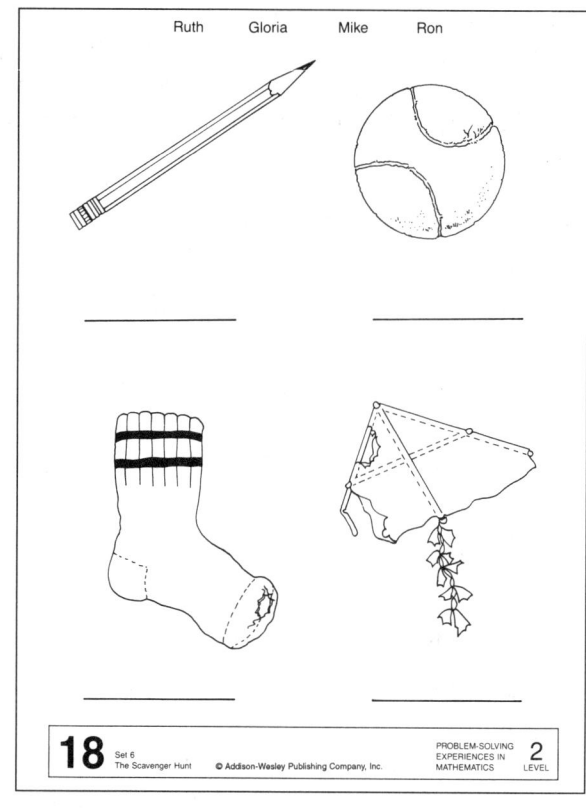

Related Problems: 20, 19, 7

Problem Extension

Suppose Ron found something to keep rain off. Gloria found something people read. What Mike found would float in a pond. And what Ruth found used to tell time, but it doesn't anymore. Which thing was not found by the children on their scavenger hunt? (*tennis racket*)

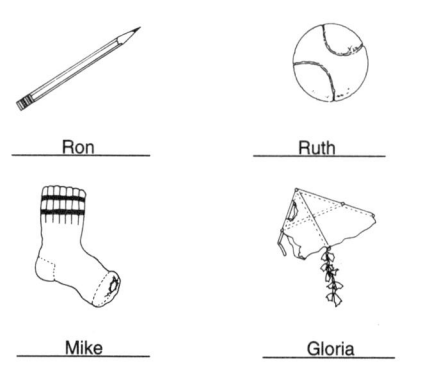

> **STRATEGY ASSESSMENT IDEAS**
>
> Listen and watch as students work to see if they
>
> - use a plan to record their work on the picture
> - correctly uses all conditions given in the problem
> - arrive at correct conclusions through reasoning

34

24 > PROCESS PROBLEM

Ruth and Mike had 7 things to find for the scavenger hunt. When the hunt was over, they had found all but one thing. Use the information to decide which thing they did not find.

Ruth said, "We found all the things that are either circles or squares." Mike said, "We found all the things that are shaped like a triangle." They also found one thing that people read.

MATERIALS

attribute blocks (1 set per group); alternatively, use other objects that are in the shapes of circles, triangles, squares, and nonsquare rectangles (2 of each shape per group)

Understanding the Problem

- How many things did Ruth and Mike have to find for the scavenger hunt? (*7*)
- Did they find all 7 things? (*no, all but one*)
- What were they trying to find? (*which thing they did not find*)
- Is the cassette tape a square? (*no, it is shaped like a rectangle, but it isn't a square*)

Solving the Problem

Use Logical Reasoning

- Is the item they did not find a triangle? (*no*) How do you know? (*Mike said they found all the triangular shapes*)
- What information do you know about the items that are circles or squares? (*they found all the things shaped like circles and squares*)

Use Manipulatives

- Listen to the story again. Place matching attribute block shapes on the pictures to show what items were found. Which item was not found?

Solution

Ruth said, "We found all the things that are either circles or squares." So, the missing item is not the ball, the wheel, or the postage stamp.

Mike said, "We found all the things that are shaped like a triangle." So, the missing item is not the dog tag or the earring.

The only item left is the cassette tape. It was not found.

Related Problems: 23, 20, 19, 7

Problem Extension

Sarah had 5 items to buy at the store, but she could only find 4 of them. She told her dad, "I found the tennis ball and the thing that has all of its sides the same." She also found the other two items that would roll. Which item did she not find? (*box of cereal*)

STRATEGY ASSESSMENT IDEAS

Listen and watch as students work to see if they

- use a plan to record their work or to place blocks on the pictures
- correctly use all conditions given in the problem
- arrive at correct conclusions through reasoning

At the Roller Rink

A new roller rink opened last week in Kim's city. It was called the Coliseum Roller Rink, and it was supposed to be the largest one in the state. Kim asked her father to take her skating the first chance he had.

On Saturday, Kim, her father, and Kim's friend Joannie went to the new skating rink. Both Kim and Joannie had their own skates, but Kim's father had to rent his. Kim and Joannie skated to every record the entire 3 hours they were at the roller rink. Kim's father skated to almost every record, but sometimes he sat down to rest.

Three times during the time they were at the Roller Rink, they had a couples-only skate. For the first one, Kim and Joannie skated together. But for the other two, Kim and her father skated together, while Joannie skated with Merisa, the skating teacher. Kim liked skating with her dad. It made her dad very happy, too.

Discussion Questions

1. What opened in Kim's city? (*a new roller rink*)
2. What did Kim ask her father? (*to take her skating*)
3. Did just Kim and her father go skating? (*no*)
4. How do you think Kim and Joannie got their own skates?
5. What is a couples-only skate? (*people skate in pairs*)
6. Why was Kim's father happy? (*he liked skating with Kim*)
7. How long could you skate at a roller rink?
8. Can you tell about what a roller skating rink near you is like?

25 SKILL ACTIVITY

Tell an Addition Question

Story A
Four boys and 8 girls held hands and made a long skaters' chain.

Possible Question for Story A
Altogether, how many boys and girls made the skaters' chain? *(12)*

Story B
Seven couples skated during the first couples-only skate. Nine other couples skated during the second couples-only skate.

Possible Question for Story B
What is the total number of couples that skated for the two couples-only skates? *(16)*

TEACHING ACTIONS

1. Read Story A to the students.
2. Have them tell a question that can be answered using data in Story A and using addition.
3. Repeat for Story B.
4. (*optional*) Have students answer their questions.

26 ONE-STEP PROBLEM

Eight skaters were holding hands and skating backward around the rink. When they started skating fast, three of the skaters let go. How many kept holding hands and skating backward?

MATERIALS

counters (at least 8 per group)

Understanding the Problem

- How many skaters were holding hands and skating backward? (*8*)
- Why do you think they were holding hands and skating backward?
- What happened when they started skating fast? (*3 let go*) Why do you think they let go?
- What are we trying to find out about the skaters? (*how many kept holding hands and skating backward*)

Planning a Solution

- Is letting go a "put together" action or a "take away" action? (*take away*)
- If 3 people were skating and 2 fell down, how many did not fall down? (*1*) Which operation did you use to find out? (*subtraction*)
- Could you use counters to show 8 skaters and then show what happened? (*see solution*)
- Can you draw a picture of 8 skaters and show what happened?

Solution

Choose the Operation

$8 - 3 = 5$ or $\begin{array}{r} 8 \\ -3 \\ \hline 5 \end{array}$

Five skaters kept holding hands and skating backward.

Draw a Picture/Use Manipulatives

5 left skating

Problem Extensions

1. Suppose 5 skaters let go. How many kept holding hands? ($8 - 5 = 3$)
2. Suppose only 2 skaters let go. How many kept holding hands? ($8 - 2 = 6$)

27 PROCESS PROBLEM

Merisa is the roller blade teacher at the Coliseum Roller Rink. She has two pairs of roller blades. One pair is black and the other is blue. She has two pairs of laces to wear with her skates. One pair is yellow and one is pink. How many ways can Merisa wear laces and skates (if Merisa makes her feet look alike)?

MATERIALS

blue, black, yellow, and pink interlocking cubes (1 of each color per group); crayons or markers in the same colors (may be used without the cubes if appropriate)

Understanding the Problem

- What does Merisa do at the roller rink? (*teaches skating*)
- How many pairs of roller blades does she have? (*2*) What colors are they? (*black and blue*) Color the roller blades on your paper.
- How many pairs of laces does Merisa have? (*2*) What colors are they? (*yellow and pink*) Color the laces on your paper.
- Does she wear two different color roller blades at the same time? (*no*) Two different color laces at the same time? (*no*)
- How many different ways can she wear the different color roller blades and the different color laces? (*4*)

Solving the Problem

Complete an Organized List

- If Merisa wears the black roller blades, what are her choices for laces? (*yellow and pink*) Pick one of the colors and write it on the list on your paper.
- Black roller blades and yellow laces is one way to dress. Can you name other ways?

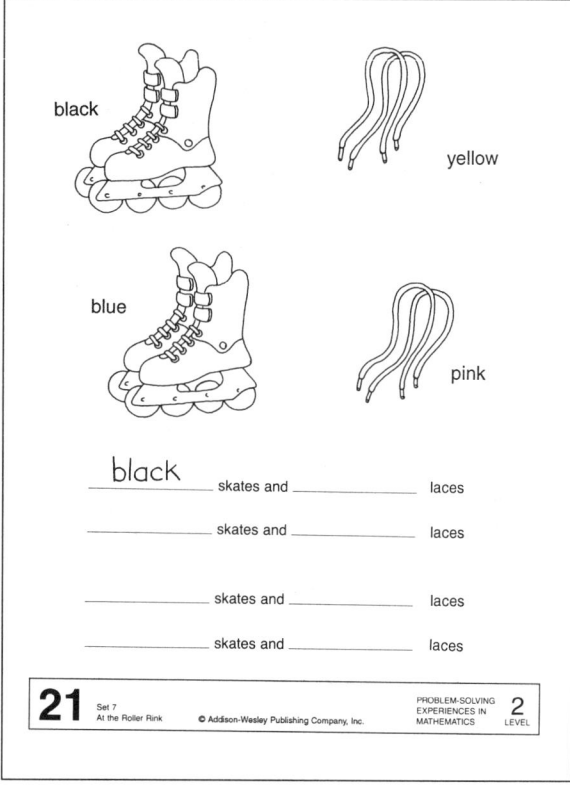

Use Manipulatives

- Place cubes on the pictures to represent colors of the roller blades and laces.
- If Merisa wears the black roller blades, what color laces can she wear? (*yellow and pink*) Use the cubes to make one of these pairs, and then record by writing the colors in the spaces. Can you show all the possible ways?

STRATEGY ASSESSMENT IDEAS

Listen and watch as students work to see if they

- create correct entries for their lists
- organize entries in their lists
- list all possibilities
- draw an appropriate picture to solve the problem (if a picture is drawn)

Solution

 black skates and yellow laces
 black skates and pink   laces

 blue skates and yellow laces
 blue skates and pink   laces

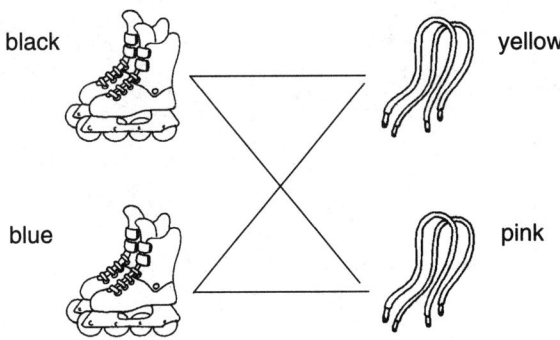

Related Problems: 20, 19, 7, 4, 3

Problem Extensions

1. What if Merisa did not always make her feet look alike? How many ways could she wear the roller blades and laces? (*both black; both blue; one black and one blue*)

2. If Merisa also has orange laces, how many different way can Merisa now wear her roller blades and laces? (*6*)

28 PROCESS PROBLEM

The Coliseum Roller Rink has races every Wednesday night. They set up a race course. Each person has to skate from the starting point to the ending point 6 times, following a different path each time. The person with the fastest time for all 6 trips is the winner. Can you list the 6 different ways to go from the start to the end?

Understanding the Problem

- What does the roller rink have on Wednesday nights? (*races*)
- Where is the starting point? (*see Blackline Master 22*) The ending point?
- How many different ways can a skater go from the starting point to the ending point? (*6*)
- Which path numbers are between the starting point and the bridge? (*1, 2, and 3*) Between the bridge and the end? (*4 and 5*)
- Does a skater have to go over the bridge? (*yes*)

Solving the Problem

- Suppose a skater took path 1 first. Which path could the skater then take on the other side of the bridge? (*4 or 5*) Write down one trip the skater could make. Then write down another trip the skater could make. (*see solution*)
- If one skater takes path 2 and then path 4, what is another trip the skater could take if the skater first took path 2? (*2 then 5*)

Solution

Complete an Organized List

first 1 then 4	first 2 then 4	first 3 then 4
first 1 then 5	first 2 then 5	first 3 then 5

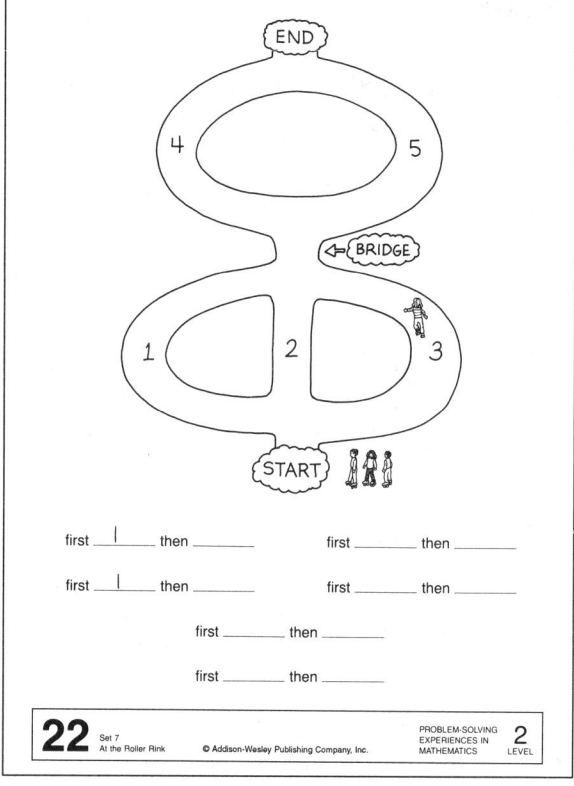

Related Problems: 27, 7, 4, 3

Problem Extension

Suppose there were 3 paths between the bridge and the end. (Have students draw another path.) Now how many different trips could a skater take from the start to the end? (*3 more or 9 in all*)

STRATEGY ASSESSMENT IDEAS

Listen and watch as students work to see if they

- create correct entries for their lists
- organize entries in their lists
- list all possibilities

The Post Office

Luis had just returned home from his visit to his grandparents, and he was anxious to tell his mom and dad about all the wonderful places they took him. "One day we went to the zoo and saw monkeys, lions, tigers, and elephants," Luis said excitedly. "On another day we took a trip to a museum. The best part about the museum was the dinosaurs. I hope I get to go and see Grandma and Grandpa again soon."

Luis's mother said, "It's wonderful that you had such a good time. I bet they'd like to get a letter from you saying what a good time you had." Luis thought so, too. In fact, the very first thing he did when he woke up the next morning was to sit down at a table and write a thank-you letter to his grandparents.

After breakfast Luis showed his mother his letter and asked her for an envelope to put it in. After he put the letter in the envelope, sealed it, and wrote his grandparents' address on the envelope, he thought the letter was ready to be mailed. "There is one other thing to do," said Mother. "You must put a stamp on the envelope. Without a stamp the letter can't be delivered. We'll have to go to the post office and get a stamp; then your letter will be ready to be mailed."

Luis and his mother walked to the post office. Luis's mother asked the clerk to show them the different kinds of stamps they could choose from. Luis could hardly believe his eyes. You could buy stamps in large sheets or in rolls. You could buy stamps with a picture of an American flag and stamps in honor of famous people or places. Luis decided that one day he would collect stamps and try to get as many different kinds of stamps as he could.

Discussion Questions

1. Who had Luis been to visit? (*his grandparents*)
2. Where did Luis go with his grandparents? (*zoo, museum*)
3. When did Luis write a letter to his grandparents? (*the morning after he got back*)

4. Why does an address need to be written on a letter?
5. Why do you have to put a stamp on a letter? (*without a stamp, the letter cannot be delivered*)
6. Was there only one kind of stamp to buy at the post office? (*no*)
7. If you collected stamps, what pictures on them would be your favorite?

29 SKILL ACTIVITY

Tell an Addition Question for a Story

Story A
When Luis and his mom went to the post office, they bought 7 stamps with space shuttles on them and 9 stamps with pictures of eagles.

Story B
Luis went to the zoo with his grandparents. He saw 7 monkeys, 3 lions, and 4 elephants.

Note (Story B): Students may suggest a 2-step addition question (for example, How many animals did Luis see at the zoo?) They may have never seen a 2-step story problem. If you ask them to answer their questions, be sure to point out that 2 additions are needed.

TEACHING ACTIONS
1. Read and discuss Story A.
2. Ask students to think of a question that can be answered using addition.
3. Repeat for Story B.
4. (*optional*) Have students answer their questions.

30 ONE-STEP PROBLEM

Ms. Potter is a mail carrier. In fact, she brings mail to Luis's house almost every day. One day she brought 8 letters and 5 small packages. How many more letters did she bring than packages?

MATERIALS

pieces of scrap paper (to represent letters; at least 8 per group); counters (to represent packages; at least 5 per group)

Understanding the Problem

- What is Ms. Potter's job? (*mail carrier*)
- What does a mail carrier do?
- How many letters did Ms. Potter bring to Luis's house? (*8*) How many packages? (*5*)
- Are we trying to find how many letters and packages Ms. Potter brought? (*no, how many more letters she brought than packages*)

Solving the Problem

- Could you let pieces of paper stand for letters and counters for packages? (*yes*)
- Is this an addition story or a subtraction story? (*subtraction*)
- Can you compare the number of letters and the number of packages? (*see solution*)
- Can you write a subtraction number sentence for this problem?

Solution

Use Subtraction (comparison type)

$8 - 5 = 3$ or $\begin{array}{r} 8 \\ -5 \\ \hline 3 \end{array}$

Ms. Potter brought 3 more letters than packages.

Use Manipulatives

□ □ □ □ □ (□ □ □)
            ↑
        3 more letters

▱ ▱ ▱ ▱ ▱

Related Problem: 26

Problem Extension

Luis plans to send letters to 11 friends. On Monday he mailed 7 of the letters. How many more letters does he have still to send? (*4*) (*Note:* This is a subtraction—missing addend problem.)

31 ▶ PROCESS PROBLEM

Luis bought 3 stamps at the post office. He bought 5¢ stamps and 4¢ stamps. He spent a total of 14¢. How many 5¢ stamps and how many 4¢ stamps did Luis buy? Draw rings around the stamps he bought.

MATERIALS

pennies or counters (14 per pair)

Understanding the Problem

- How many stamps did Luis buy at the post office? *(3)*
- Did all 3 stamps cost the same amount? *(no, some cost 5¢ and some cost 4¢)*
- How much money did he spend in all? *(14¢)*
- Did he buy only 5¢ stamps? *(no)*

Solving the Problem

Guess and Check

- Did Luis buy 4 stamps? *(no)* Which pictures of stamps are possible? *(only those with 3 stamps)*
- Try any of the sets of 3 stamps to see if they give the correct amount.
- Did you choose the correct set? If not, were you too low or too high? Try again!

Use Manipulatives

- Use the pennies and the picture to help you figure out which stamps Luis bought. Look at one of the groups of stamps. Stack the amount of pennies that Luis had to pay for each stamp on top of that stamp. Did you use all 14 pennies? Fewer than 14? Would it take more than 14? Which picture shows the stamps that Luis bought?

Solution

All the pictures with 4 stamps can be crossed out.

4 ¢ + 4 ¢ + 5 ¢ = 13 ¢ *(too low)*

5 ¢ + 5 ¢ + 4 ¢ = 14 ¢ *(correct)*

(Alternatively, try each combination of stamps until the answer is found.)

Related Problems: 24, 23, 20, 19, 8

Problem Extension

Luis bought 3 stamps at the post office. He bought some 3¢ stamps and some 2¢ stamps. He spent a total of 8¢. How many 3¢ stamps and 2¢ stamps did he buy?

STRATEGY ASSESSMENT IDEAS

Listen and watch as students work to see if they

- make a reasonable first guess (the pictures with 4 stamps should not be used)
- make a second guess using what they learn from checking their first guess
- use pennies to check their guesses

32 PROCESS PROBLEM

One day Luis addressed 3 letters. He put one stamp on each letter. The stamps cost a total of 13¢. Which stamps did he put on the 3 letters? Draw rings around the letters he addressed.

Understanding the Problem

- How many letters did Luis address? (*3*)
- Did he have to put stamps on the envelopes? (*yes*)
- How much did the stamps cost? (*13¢*)
- Are we trying to find how many letters Luis addressed? (*no, we know he addressed 3; we want to know which stamps he put on the letters*)

Solving the Problem

- Can you find 3 numbers that add up to 13¢?
- Could 4¢, 5¢, and 6¢ be the stamps? (*no*) Why not? (*sum is 15¢, not 13¢*)
- How much too high is 4 + 5 + 6? (*2¢ too high*) How can we make the sum 13? (*take away 2¢*)
- Could Luis have put the same amount on 2 of the letters? (*yes*)
- If 2 stamps were the same, what would the third stamp have to be? (*see solution*)

Solution

Guess and Check

4¢ + 5¢ + 6¢ = 15¢ (*too high by 2¢*)
4¢ + 5¢ + 4¢ = 13¢ (*correct*)
    or
4¢ + 4¢ + 4¢ = 12¢ (*close but 1¢ low*)
4¢ + 4¢ + 5¢ = 13¢ (*correct*)

The third stamp would have to be a 5¢ stamp.

Related Problems: 31, 8, 7

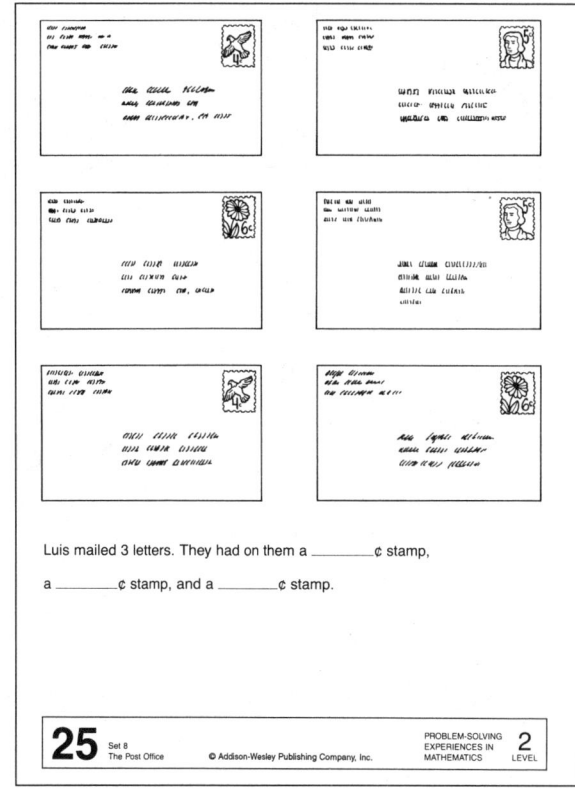

Problem Extension

One day Luis addressed 3 letters. He put one stamp on each letter. The stamps cost a total of 9¢. Which stamps did he put on the 3 letters? (*3¢ stamp on each letter*)

STRATEGY ASSESSMENT IDEAS

Listen and watch as students work to see if they

- make a reasonable first guess (student must select 3 stamps)
- make a second guess using what they learn from checking the first guess

47

SET 9

Future Dreams

Lisa liked to dream about what she would be when she grew up. Sometimes, after she finished her homework, she would sit outside by a tree and imagine all the things she could do.

One day, Lisa imaged herself as a ballerina. She dreamed she was twirling in the center of the stage and smiling when the crowd applauded. In Lisa's dream, she felt like she could dance forever.

Then Lisa dreamed that she was a famous piano player. She imagined how excited she would feel sitting by a piano, getting ready to play a sweet melody. As a piano player, Lisa thought, she could also teach others how to play.

Lisa also dreamed about becoming a diver, since she liked to swim so much. In her dream, Lisa imagined herself standing on the tallest diving board at the pool. She would raise her arms and jump high into the air. Then she would do somersaults in the air and finish with a perfect dive into the water.

Lisa did not sit by the tree for a long time. She knew that if she wanted to become the things she dreamed about, she needed to practice. She ran into the house to ask her mom if she could take diving lessons.

Discussion Questions

1. What did Lisa like to dream about? (*what she would be when she grew up*)
2. Where would she sometimes go to dream? (*outside by a tree*)
3. What are some things you like to dream about?
4. In Lisa's dream of becoming a ballerina, how long did she think she could dance? (*forever*)
5. Was Lisa already a piano player? (*no*)
6. Could Lisa already swim? (*yes*)
7. What did Lisa ask her mom when she ran into the house? (*if she could take diving lessons*)

33 SKILL ACTIVITY

Tell an Addition Question

Picture A

Five children are swimming in a stream. Three children are on the bank watching the 5 children.

Questions for Picture A

1. How many children are swimming? (*5*)
2. How many children are not swimming? (*3*)

Picture B

Lisa is looking at several pairs of ballet slippers. Four pairs are in one group, three pairs in another, and five pairs in another.

Note: Picture A suggests a straightforward addition question: "How many children are there in all?" In discussion, emphasize that in addition we "put together" even though the picture does not show the action.

Questions for Picture B

Note: Before asking the questions, have students color the slippers on the hooks blue, slippers on the floor red, and slippers on the table yellow.

1. How many pairs of slippers are blue? (*4*)
2. How many pairs of slippers are red? (*3*)
3. How many pairs of slippers are yellow? (*5*)

Note: Picture B is more complex than Picture A. First, be sure students understand what pair means. Be sure they have colored the slippers properly before asking them to make up questions. There are several possible questions (for example, "How may blue and red slippers are there?" "How many blue and yellow slippers are there?" "How many slippers does Lisa have in all?").

TEACHING ACTIONS

1. Show and discuss Picture A.
2. Read the questions to accompany Picture A.
3. Have students tell an addition question related to the picture.
4. Discuss the students' addition questions.
5. Repeat for Picture B.
6. (*optional*) Have students give answers to their addition questions.

34 ONE-STEP PROBLEM

Lisa wanted to learn how to play the piano, so she took piano lessons. In the first week she learned how to play 7 songs on the piano. The next week she learned 11 songs. How many songs did Lisa learn to play on the piano in 2 weeks?

Understanding the Problem

- What did Lisa do to learn how to play the piano? (*took piano lessons*)
- How many piano songs did she learn the first week? (*7*) The second week? (*11*)
- What do we want to find? (*how many piano songs Lisa learned in 2 weeks*)

Solving the Problem

- Can you write a number sentence for this story? (*see solution*)
- Is this an addition story or a subtraction story? (*addition*)
- If Lisa learned only 2 piano songs one week and 3 piano songs the next week, how many songs did she learn? (*5*) Now can you do the problem if she learned 7 songs and 11 songs?

Solution

Choose the Operation

- Use addition: $7 + 11 = 18$ or $\begin{array}{r} 7 \\ + 11 \\ \hline 18 \end{array}$

Lisa learned 18 piano songs in the 2 weeks.

Related Problems: 22, 18

Problem Extension

Lisa learned 8 piano songs in one week and 12 piano songs in the next week. How many more songs did she learn in the second week than in the first? ($12 - 8 = 4$)

35 PROCESS PROBLEM

Lisa plays for the Hurrying Hippos baseball team. During the baseball season, her team plays a team called the Lions 6 times. So far, the Lions have won each of the first 4 games. If you look at the chart closely, you will see that the scores follow a pattern. If both teams continue to score runs as they did in the first 4 games, what will the scores be in the last 2 games? Which team will win these 2 games?

MATERIALS

interlocking cubes (at least 15 per pair)

Understanding the Problem

- What is the name of Lisa's baseball team? (*Hurrying Hippos*)
- How many times does her team play the Lions team? (*6 times*)
- Which team won the first 4 games? (*Lions*)
- What was the score in game 1? (*Hippos 1, Lions 5*)
- What was the score in game 4? (*Hippos 10, Lions 11*)

Solving the Problem

Look for a Pattern

- How many more runs did the Hippos make in game 2 than game 1? (*3*) Game 3 than game 2? (*3*) Game 4 than game 3? (*3*) Now how many more runs did they score in game 5 than game 4? (*3*)
- How many more runs did the Lions make in game 2 than game 1? (*2*) Game 3 than game 2? (*2*) Game 4 than game 3? (*2*) Now, how many more runs did they score in game 5 than 4? (*2*)

- What scores did the Hippos make in the first 4 games? (*1, 4, 7, and 10*) Do you see a pattern? (*increase by 3 each time*) What score will they make in game 5? (*13*) Game 6? (*16*)
- What scores did the Lions make in the first 4 games? (*5, 7, 9, and 11*) Do you see a pattern? (*increase by 2 each time*) What score will they make in game 5? (*13*) Game 6? (*15*)
- Who won game 5? (*tie*) Game 6? (*Hippos*)

STRATEGY ASSESSMENT IDEAS

Listen and watch as students work to see if they

- describe a pattern shown in the table
- extend the pattern correctly
- use the pattern to arrive at the correct answer

Use Manipulatives

- Use cubes to represent the number of runs made by the Hippos in game 1. How many more cubes would you need to add to show the number of runs for game 2? (*3*) How many for game 3? (*3*)
- Do you see a pattern? (*increases by 3 each time*)
- Repeat with the Lions scores. (*increases by 2 each time*)
- What score will the Hippos make in game 5? (*13*) The Lions? (*13*) How about game 6?

Solution

Hippos' pattern: increase by 3 every game, so the pattern is 1, 4, 7, 10, 13, 16

Lions' pattern: increase by 2 every game, so the pattern is 5, 7, 9, 11, 13, 15

Game 5 was a tie (13–13). Game 6 was won by the Hippos (16–15).

Related Problems: 16, 15, 12, 11

Problem Extension

Suppose the Hurrying Hippos baseball team played 6 games against the Marvelous Monkeys. The scores for the first 4 games are shown in the chart. The scores follow a pattern. What will the scores be for games 5 and 6?

	Game 1	Game 2	Game 3	Game 4	Game 5	Game 6
Hippos	1	4	7	10	13	16
Lions	5	7	9	11	13	15

36 PROCESS PROBLEM

Lisa likes to dress one of her stuffed animals, a hippopotamus, in a ballet costume called a tutu and ballet slippers. Lisa has 2 tutus for her stuffed animal, 1 red and 1 blue. She also has 3 colors of ballet slippers—red, blue, and yellow. Lisa made a record of what she dressed her stuffed hippo in for 5 days. Can you help Lisa decide how to dress the hippo for the next 2 days?

Note: Have students color the tutus and the slippers for the first 5 days as follows: tutus—red, blue, red, blue, red; and slippers—red, blue, yellow, red, blue.

Understanding the Problem

- What does Lisa put on her stuffed animal hippo? (*tutu and ballet slippers*)
- How many tutus does Lisa have to put on the stuffed hippo? (2) What colors? (*red and blue*)
- How many pairs of ballet slippers does Lisa use? (3) What colors? (*red, blue, yellow*)
- What color tutu and what color slippers did Lisa use for Sunday (day 1)? (*red tutu and red slippers*)
- What color tutu and what color slippers did Lisa use for Thursday (day 5)? (*red tutu and blue slippers*)

Solving the Problem

- Can you decide what color tutu Lisa will put on the stuffed hippo for Friday (day 6)? (*blue*) Lisa used red, blue, red, blue, red—what color comes next? (*blue*) Color it in.
- Can you decide what color slippers Lisa will use for Friday (day 6)? (*yellow*) Lisa used red, blue, yellow, red, blue—what color comes next? (*yellow*) Color it in.
- Now can you decide what Lisa will use on Saturday (day 7)?

Solution

Look for a Pattern

Pattern for tutus: red, blue, red, blue, red, blue, red

Pattern for slippers: red, blue, yellow, red, blue, yellow, red

Lisa put a blue tutu and yellow slippers on her stuffed hippo for Friday and a red tutu and red slippers for Saturday.

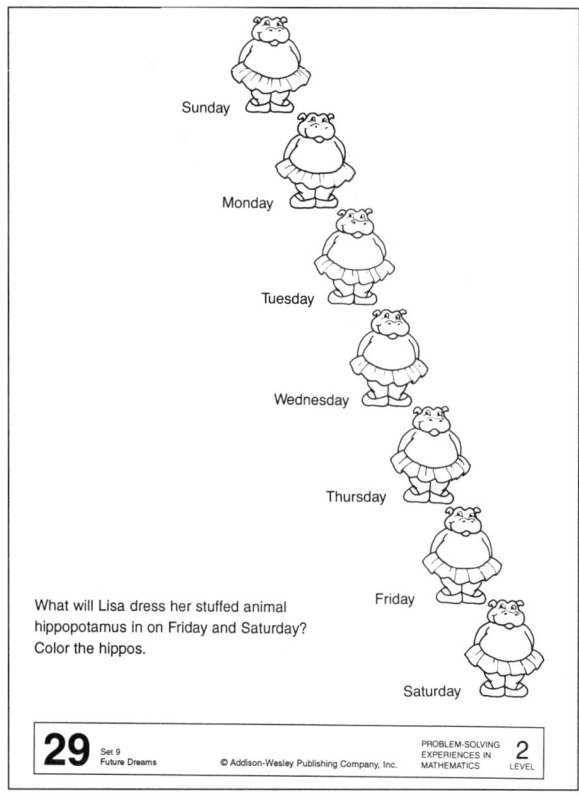

What will Lisa dress her stuffed animal hippopotamus in on Friday and Saturday? Color the hippos.

Related Problems: 35, 16, 15, 12, 11

Problem Extension

	Sunday	Monday	Tuesday	Wednesday	Thursday	Friday	Saturday
Tutu	red	red	blue	red	red		
Slippers	blue	yellow	red	blue	yellow		

Lisa never puts the same color tutu and ballet slippers on her stuffed hippo. The chart shows what Lisa put on her stuffed hippo for 5 days. Complete the pattern to find what Lisa put on her stuffed hippo for next 2 days. (*Friday—blue tutu, red slippers; Saturday—red tutu, blue slippers*)

STRATEGY ASSESSMENT IDEAS

Listen and watch as students work to see if they

- describe the patterns
- extend the patterns correctly
- use the patterns to arrive at the correct answer

SET 10

Johnny Appleseed

Have you ever heard of John Chapman? Probably not. But have you ever heard of Johnny Appleseed? Well, Johnny Appleseed was a real person and his real name was John Chapman. John Chapman lived almost 200 years ago. He got the name Johnny Appleseed because he spent 40 years walking through the states of Ohio and Indiana planting apple seeds. Back then the frontier people didn't have much fruit to eat, so Johnny wanted to help his friends by planting apple trees.

Johnny Appleseed was a rough and tough frontier traveler. His long hair touched his shoulders and kept him warm in the winter. The stories about Johnny Appleseed say that he never wore shoes, even in the snow! He walked barefoot through the forest until his feet were so tough he could walk on ice and it didn't hurt.

When Johnny Appleseed visited a town, he always stopped to tell children frontier stories. Usually the stories were about himself. Johnny Appleseed was also known for his kindness to animals. Whenever he saw a sick animal, he always tried to help it get better.

Now you know that John Chapman was the real name of a famous American.

Discussion Questions

1. Was Johnny Appleseed a real person? (*yes*)
2. Was Johnny Appleseed his real name? (*no*)
3. How did he get the name Johnny Appleseed? (*he spend 40 years planting apple seeds*)
4. What kind of fruit tree would you plant if you had a choice?
5. If Johnny planted oranges instead of apples, what name would you have given him?

37 SKILL ACTIVITY

Tell Why an Answer Is Not Reasonable

Problem A

Johnny has 7 seeds in a bag. He has 4 seeds in another bag. How many seeds does he have altogether in the 2 bags?

Unreasonable Answer for Problem A

6 seeds

Problem B

Johnny had 11 seeds in his bag. He planted 5 seeds. How many seeds did he have left to plant if he wanted to plant them all?

Unreasonable Answer for Problem B

16 seeds

TEACHING ACTIONS

1. Read Problem A to the students. Do not have them solve the problem.
2. Have students tell why the answer given is not reasonable.
3. Repeat for Problem B.
4. (*optional*) Have students solve each problem.

38 > ONE-STEP PROBLEM

Johnny Appleseed was determined to plant 13 apple seeds one day. By lunch time, he had planted 8 apple seeds. How many more did he need to plant before the day ended?

Understanding the Problem

- What does it mean to be "determined"?
- How many apple seeds did Johnny want to plant in one day? (*13*)
- What does "by the end of the day" mean?
- Did he get all 13 planted by lunch time? (*no*) How many did he get planted? (*8*)
- What are we trying to find? (*how many more apple seeds Johnny Appleseed needs to plant before the day is over*)

Solving the Problem

- If you wanted to plant 4 seeds and you have only planted 1, how many more do you need to plant? (*3*) Which operation could you have used to find that answer? (*subtraction*)
- Are you trying to find the total number of seeds he planted in one day? (*no*)
- Do you know how many he planted before lunch? (*yes, 8*) Do you know how many he planted after lunch? (*no*) Do you know how many he planted in all? (*yes, 13*) Can you add or subtract to find the missing number? (*subtract*)
- Can you draw a picture to find how many more seeds he needs to plant?

Solution

Choose the Operation

$$13 - 8 = 5 \quad \text{or} \quad \begin{array}{r} 13 \\ -\ 8 \\ \hline 5 \end{array}$$

He must plant 5 more seeds.

Draw a Picture

○○○○○ ○○○ ○○○○○
 _____ _____
  8 planted   5 more to plant

Note: The problem is a missing addend subtraction situation. It could be set up as 8 + ? = 13. Some students may want to count on to find the missing addend.

Related Problems: 30, 26

Problem Extensions

1. Suppose Johnny Appleseed planted only 5 seeds before lunch. How many more did he need to plant? (*13 − 5 = 8*)
2. Suppose 4 of the 13 seeds grew into trees. How many did not grow into trees? (*13 − 4 = 9*)

39 > PROCESS PROBLEM

One day Johnny Appleseed was walking on a river bank. Up ahead he saw 5 beautiful fields, but they were not as beautiful as they could be, because there were no apple trees! Johnny planted 4 seeds in the first field, 8 seeds in the second, 12 seeds in the third, and so on. If Johnny kept planting seeds in this pattern, how many seeds did he plant in the fifth field?

MATERIALS

counters or popcorn kernels to represent apple seeds (at least 20 per group)

Understanding the Problem

- What did Johnny Appleseed see when he was walking on a river bank? (*5 beautiful fields*)
- Why weren't the fields as beautiful as they could be? (*there were no apple trees in them*)
- What did Johnny Appleseed do in the first field? (*he planted 4 seeds*) The second field? (*he planted 8 seeds*) The third field? (*he planted 12 seeds*)
- What are we trying to find? (*how many seeds he planted in the fifth field*)

Solving the Problem

Complete a Table/Look for a Pattern

- What are the numbers in the top row of the table? (*the number of the field*)
- What are the numbers in the bottom row? (*the number of seeds planted in each field*)
- Do you see a pattern in the number of seeds planted?
- Can you find how many seeds Johnny Appleseed planted in field 4? (*16*) Count by 4s.

Number of the Field	1	2	3	4	5
Number of Seeds Planted in the Field					

Use Manipulatives

- With your counters, show how many seeds Johnny Appleseed planted in the first field. Point to where this information is located on your table.
- How many more counters do you need to show how many seeds he planted in the second field? (*4*) How many more counters do you need to show how many seeds he planted in the third field? (*4*) How many more counters will you need to show how many seeds he planted in the fourth field? (*4*) Fifth field? (*4*) What pattern do you see? (*multiples of 4*)
- Complete the table using this information.

STRATEGY ASSESSMENT IDEAS

Listen and watch as students work to see if they

- place counters correctly in the table
- use a pattern to correctly extend the table
- interpret the table to arrive at the correct answer

Solution

Number of the Field	1	2	3	4	5
Number of Seeds Planted in the Field	4	8	12	16	20

Johnny Appleseed planted 20 seeds in the fifth field.

Related Problems: 36, 35, 16, 15, 12

Problem Extension

Suppose there were more fields and Johnny Appleseed kept planting seeds in the same pattern. In which field would he plant 32 seeds? (*field 8*)

40 PROCESS PROBLEM

Even though Johnny Appleseed planted apple trees, he didn't have an apple tree of his own. So, whenever he went to the grocery store, be bought some apples. How much did Johnny Appleseed have to pay for 6 apples?

MATERIALS

pennies or counters (at least 12 per group)

Understanding the Problem

- Why did Johnny Appleseed have to buy apples? (*he didn't have any apple trees of his own*)
- How much did the apples cost? (*2¢ each*)
- Does it matter how big the apple was? (*no, they all cost 2¢*)
- How many apples did Johnny buy? (*6*)

Solving the Problem

Complete a Table/Look for a Pattern

- What does the top row of numbers in the table show? (*the number of apples bought*) The bottom row of numbers? (*the total cost for the apples*)
- How much does it cost to buy 2 apples? (*4¢*) Point to the place that shows this in the table.
- Can you use the table to tell how much it costs to buy 3 apples? (*yes, 6¢*)
- Count by 2s. Look at the cost for the apples. Do you see a pattern? (*multiples of 2*)
- How much does it cost to buy 4 apples? Can you add 2¢ to 6¢ to find out? (*6¢ + 2¢ = 8¢*)
- Can you use pennies to find the cost of 6 apples?

Solution

Number of Apples	1	2	3	4	5	6
Cost	2¢	4¢	6¢	8¢	10¢	12¢

Johnny Appleseed paid 12¢ for 6 apples.

Related Problems: 39, 36, 35, 16, 15

Problem Extension

Johnny Appleseed had 20¢. How many apples could he buy? (*10 apples*)

Note: For this extension, some students may extend the table to 10 apples. Some may notice that 5 cost 10¢, so 10 would cost 20¢.

STRATEGY ASSESSMENT IDEAS

Listen and watch as students work to see if they

- place numbers correctly in the table
- use a pattern to correctly extend the table
- interpret the table to arrive at the correct answer

SET 11

Summer Friends

For as long as Nicki can remember, she and her family have spent their summer vacations camping in the mountains. But this last summer, Nicki's family spent a week in a big house on the beach.

The day they arrived at their beach house, Nicki met two girls her age playing by the water. Their names were Raja and Fran, and their families were on vacation too.

Just after breakfast, Nicki, Raja, and Fran met by a big rock to plan what they wanted to do that day. Every day they went swimming in the ocean. And each day they did something they had not done before. One day they looked for sea shells, one day they dug for clams in the wet sand, and one day they built a sand castle.

Nicki, Raja, and Fran became best friends. They each thought their week at the beach was the best vacation they ever had. They all wanted to come back again next summer. Before they said good bye, they gave each other their addresses so they could write each other letters during the winter. They all hoped winter would go by quickly.

Discussion Questions

1. Where did Nicki's family go for vacation this last summer? (*to the beach*)
2. Had Nicki been to the beach for vacation before? (*no*)
3. Who were the girls that Nicki met at the beach? (*Raja, Fran*)
4. What types of activities did Nicki, Raja, and Fran do? (*went swimming, looked for sea shells, dug for clams, built a sand castle*)
5. What does it mean for winter to go by quickly?
6. Have you ever been to the ocean? What do you remember about the ocean and the beach?

41 SKILL ACTIVITY

Tell a Subtraction Question

Story A
Nicki's mother put 6 bathing suits in the dryer after the girls had been swimming. Later, when she opened the dryer, 2 of the bathing suits were not dry.

Possible Question for Story A
How many bathing suits were dry? (4)

Story B
Fran counted 12 seagulls sitting on the sand near her family's car. When she got close to them, 4 flew away.

Possible Question for Story B
How many seagulls did not fly away? (8)

TEACHING ACTIONS

1. Read Story A to the students.
2. Have them tell a question that can be answered using data in Story A and using subtraction.
3. Repeat for Story B.
4. (*optional*) Have students answer their questions.

42. ONE-STEP PROBLEM

Nicki, Raja, and Fran went fishing with Nicki's family. They rented a big boat and they decided to have a fishing contest. Nicki's father and brother said they could catch more fish than Nicki, Raja, Fran, and Nicki's mother altogether! Nicki's father was wrong, because at the end of the day, the girls had caught 8 fish, and the boys had only caught 6 fish. By the end of the day, how many fish did they catch altogether?

MATERIALS
counters

Understanding the Problem
- What did Nicki, Raja, and Fran do with Nicki's family? (*went fishing*)
- What did Nicki's father and brother say they would do? (*catch more fish than the girls*) Did they? (*no*)
- How many fish did the boys catch? (*6*) How many did the girls catch? (*8*)
- What are we trying to find? (*how many fish were caught altogether*)

Solving the Problem
- Are we trying to find how many more fish the girls caught than the boys? (*no*)
- To find the total number of fish, which operation should you use? (*addition*)
- Can you use counters or draw a picture to help you find the solution?

Solution
Choose the Operation

8 + 6 = 14   or   8
                  + 6

                   14

They caught 14 fish by the end of the day.

Related Problems: 34, 22, 18

Problem Extensions
1. How many more fish did the girls catch than the boys? ($8 - 6 = 2$)
2. Suppose the girls caught 12 fish instead of 8. How many more fish did the girls catch than the boys? ($12 - 6 = 6$)

43 PROCESS PROBLEM

Nicki, Raja, and Fran each filled a bag full of sea shells that they found on the beach. Nicki's father asked each of them to choose their prettiest shell. Each picked a different color shell; one was brown, one was blue, and one orange. Fran wanted to give her mother her prettiest shell because her mother's favorite color was blue. When Raja started to look in her bag for her prettiest shell, she was surprised that there weren't any orange shells. Which color shell did each girl have?

MATERIALS

crayons or markers in appropriate colors (at least brown, blue, and orange)

Understanding the Problem

- What did Nicki, Raja, and Fran each fill a bag with? (*sea shells*)
- What color were the shells? (*brown, blue, orange*) Color the shells on your paper.
- What did Nicki's father ask them to pick? (*the prettiest shell each found*)
- Did they all pick the same color shell? (*no*) What color shells were picked? (*brown, blue, orange*)
- What color shell did Fran give her mother? (*blue*)
- What didn't Raja have in her bag? (*any orange shells*)

Solving the Problem

- Can you draw a line from Fran's name to her blue shell?
- If Fran has the blue shell, can anyone else have the blue shell? (*no*)
- If Raja doesn't have an orange shell, who has to have the orange shell? (*Nicki, because Fran already has the blue shell*) Can you draw a line to show which shell Raja has?

STRATEGY ASSESSMENT IDEAS

Listen and watch as students work to see if they

- use the picture appropriately to solve the problem
- correctly uses all conditions given in the problem
- arrive at correct conclusions through reasoning

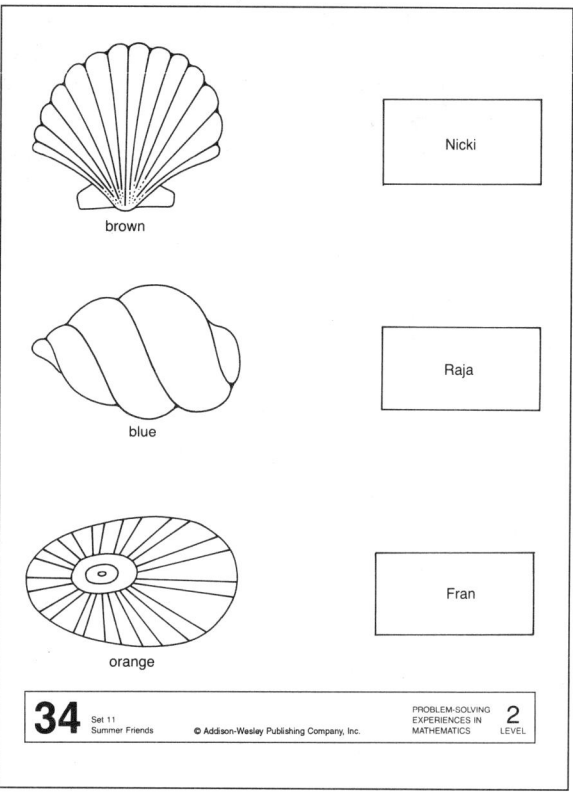

Solution

Use a Picture/Use Logical Reasoning

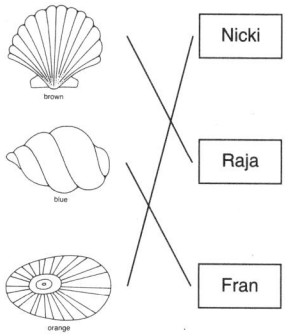

Related Problems: 31, 24, 23, 20, 19

Problem Extension

Suppose Raja found she didn't have any brown shells. Which color shell did each have? (*Nicki—brown; Raja—orange; Fran—blue*)

44 PROCESS PROBLEM

Nicki, Raja, and Fran were digging in the wet sand one day and they each found a live clam. The clams were 3 different sizes. Clams live inside hard shells. The girls tried to open the shells with their hands, but they couldn't do it. Fran found the middle-sized shell. Raja's shell was larger than Nicki's. Who found the smallest shell?

MATERIALS

crayons or markers

Understanding the Problem

- What did the girls find digging in the wet sand? (*clams*) What are clams?
- Were they all the same size? (*no, 3 different sizes*)
- Could they open their clams with their hands? (*no*)
- Who found the middle-sized shell? (*Fran*)
- Was Raja's shell larger or smaller than Nicki's? (*larger*)

Solving the Problem

- Can you draw Fran's shell?
- If Fran has a middle-sized shell, which size shells must the others be? (*one the largest and one the smallest*)
- If Raja's shell is larger than Nicki's, is hers the largest shell or the smallest shell? (*largest*) Can you draw Raja's shell?
- If Raja has the largest shell and Fran has the middle-sized shell, which shell must Nicki have? (*the smallest*)

Solution

Draw a Picture/Use Logical Reasoning

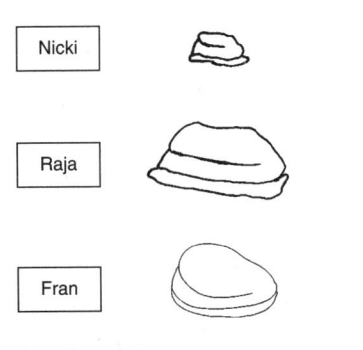

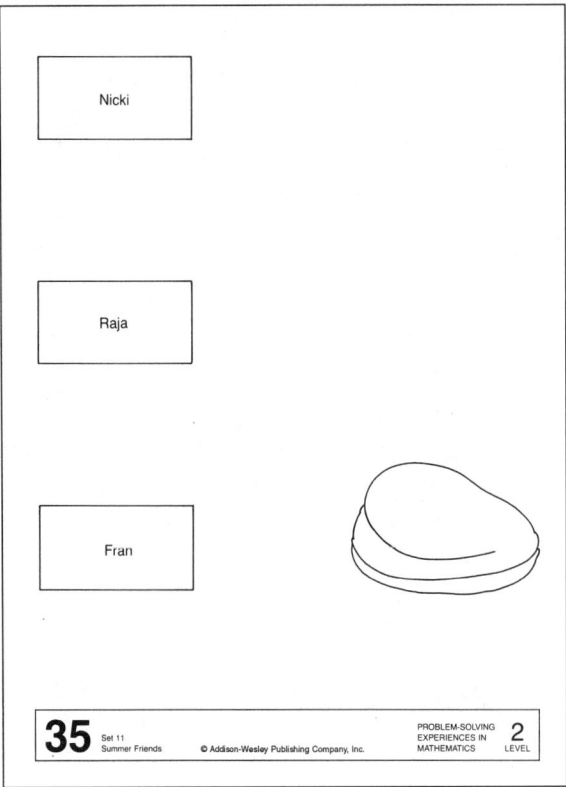

Related Problems: 43, 31, 24, 23, 20

Problem Extensions

1. Suppose Fran had the largest shell. Who would have had the middle-sized shell? (*Raja*)
2. Suppose Fran had the middle-sized shell, but Raja's shell was smaller than Nicki's. Who had the largest shell? (*Nicki*)

STRATEGY ASSESSMENT IDEAS

Listen and watch as students work to see if they

- draw appropriate pictures to solve the problem
- use the pictures appropriately to solve the problem
- correctly use all conditions given in the problem
- arrive at correct conclusions through reasoning

Life at a Pond

A pond is a pool of water, usually much smaller than a lake. A pond is a very interesting place to visit. That is, it is interesting if you like to see many kinds of animals. Of course, fish of different sizes, shapes, and colors swim in ponds. Frogs and toads also swim in or hop about near a pond. Frogs and toads look very much alike. The main difference is that frogs will usually swim in the pond, but toads will usually stay on the land near the edge of the pond.

Sometimes snakes live near ponds. Some snakes are very dangerous because they are poisonous, but most snakes that live around ponds are harmless. In fact, when snakes see people coming, they usually hide.

Turtles live in ponds, too. When turtles are on land they move very slowly, but when they are in the pond they are good swimmers. A special thing about turtles is that they carry their homes with them everywhere they go. Turtles can pull their heads and legs inside their shells whenever they want to sleep or hide.

Many animals might live in or near a pond. A few others are snails, ducks, and all sorts of insects—dragonflies, beetles, water bugs, and mosquitoes. A pond is a place full of life. If you ever visit one, keep very still for a few minutes, and you will probably see some interesting creatures.

Discussion Questions

1. Is a pond as large as a lake? (*no*)
2. Can you name some animals that live in or near a pond? (*fish, frogs, toads, snakes, turtles, snails, ducks, insects*)
3. What is special about turtles? (*they carry their homes with them*)
4. What do you think frogs and toads eat for food?
5. What usually happens when a snake sees people coming? (*they hide*)
6. What animals would you like to see if you went to a pond?

45 SKILL ACTIVITY

Tell a Subtraction Question for a Story

Story A
Seven frogs were sitting on lily pads in a pond. Suddenly 3 frogs jumped off their lily pads into the water.

Story B
Nine turtles and 6 frogs were sitting near a pond on a fine, sunny day. It had been very cold the day before, and they all wanted to let the sun warm them up.

Notes: Story A suggests a "take away" subtraction question, "How many frogs were still on the lily pads?" Story B suggest a "comparison subtraction" question, "How many more turtles were there than frogs?" Point out to students that not all subtraction questions involve take-away situations.

TEACHING ACTIONS
1. Read and discuss Story A.
2. Ask students to think of a question that can be answered using subtraction.
3. Repeat for Story B.
4. (*optional*) Have students answer their questions.

46 ONE-STEP PROBLEM

A mother duck often brings her baby ducks to the pond for a swim. The mother duck has 9 ducklings in all. One day when she and her ducklings arrived at the pond, there were only 5 ducklings. How many were missing?

Understanding the Problem

- Why does the mother duck bring her baby ducks? (*to the pond*)
- How many ducklings does the duck have? (*9*)
- Did all her ducklings follow her to the pond one day? (*no*)

Solving the Problem

- How many baby ducks are in the picture? (*5*)
- Can you draw in more ducklings to make the total number of ducklings the mother duck has?
- How many more do you have to count starting at 5 to get 9? (*4*)
- Is this an addition story or a subtraction story? (*either*)

Solution

Choose the Operation

- Use subtraction:

  $9 - 5 = 4$ or $\begin{array}{r} 9 \\ -5 \\ \hline 4 \end{array}$

  4 ducklings are missing.

- Use counting on:

  Start at 5 and count 6, 7, 8, 9. Four ducklings are missing.

- Write a missing addend number sentence: $5 + \_\_ = 9$.

  Think: "What do I add to 5 to get 9?" Answer: 4.

  Four ducklings are missing.

Related Problems: 38, 30, 26

Problem Extension

A mother duck has 9 baby ducks and a mother robin has 3 baby robins. How many more babies does the mother duck have than the mother robin? (*comparison subtraction:* $9 - 3 = 6$)

69

47 PROCESS PROBLEM

Keiko likes to visit the pond. He has named some of the animals he often sees at the pond. Some of the animals Keiko named are Sadie Snail, Freddie Frog, Reggie Robin, and Dora Duck. One day, Keiko decided to make homes of out empty cardboard boxes for these pond animals. Here are clues to help to find which box Keiko made for which animal:

Clue 1: Dora Duck doesn't get a medium-size box.
Clue 2: Freddie Frog doesn't get the largest box.
Clue 3: Reggie Robin gets a box with a bow.
Clue 4: Sadie Snail gets the smallest box.

Understanding the Problem

- What did Keiko make? (*animal homes out of empty boxes*)
- What did he name the animals? (*Sadie Snail, Freddie Frog, Reggie Robin, Dora Duck*)
- What is a clue? (*a little information to help you solve a problem*)
- Did Dora Duck get a medium-size box? (*no*)

Solving the Problem

- Who got the box with the bow? (*Reggie Robin*) Draw a line from the box to the animal.
- Which box did Sadie Snail get? (*smallest box*) Draw a line from Sadie to the box she got.
- Which boxes are left? (*largest and medium sizes*) Which animals are left? (*Freddie Frog and Dora Duck*) Can you decide which box each animal gets?
- Dora doesn't get the medium-size box. Which box is that? Which box does she get? (*largest box*)
- Now, which box is left for Freddie Frog? (*medium-size box*)

Solution

Use Logical Reasoning

Reggie gets the box with a bow. Sadie gets the smallest box. There are only 2 boxes left—the largest box and a medium-size box. Dora doesn't get a medium-size box, so she must get the largest one. Freddie gets the box that is left—the medium-size one.

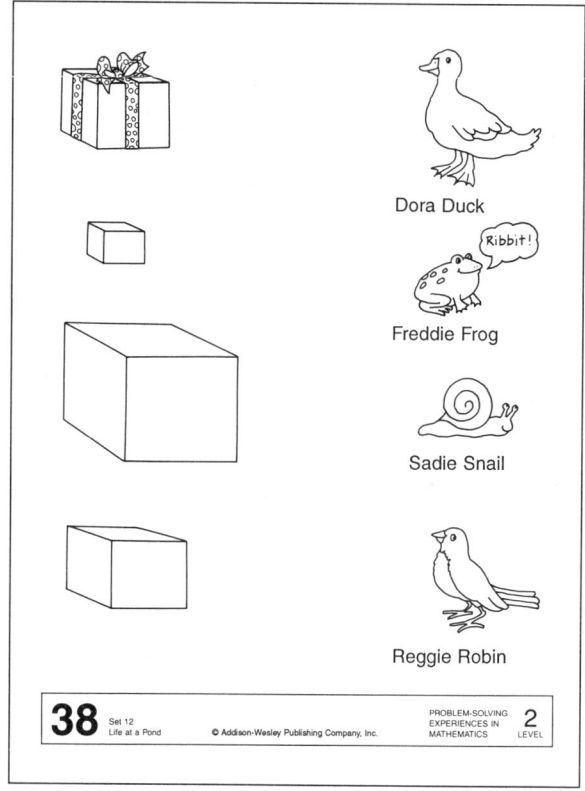

Related Problems: 44, 43, 31, 24, 23

Problem Extension

Keiko and 4 of his friends, Dan, Lupe, Antonio, and Inga, had a race. Inga didn't win, but she beat Dan and Keiko. Dan finished ahead of Keiko, and Lupe finished the race behind Antonio but ahead of Inga. Who won the race? Who finished last? (*Antonio won the race; Keiko finished last; results in order were Antonio, Lupe, Inga, Dan, Keiko*)

STRATEGY ASSESSMENT IDEAS

Listen and watch as students work to see if they

- use a plan to record their work on the picture
- correctly use all conditions given in the problem
- arrive at correct conclusions through reasoning

48 PROCESS PROBLEM

The pond Keiko visited was near a forest. Sometimes Keiko saw bear claw prints in the mud near the pond. A forest ranger told Keiko that sometimes a bear visited the pond when people were not around. The ranger gave Keiko 3 clues to guess how old the bear was. The clues were:

1. The bear is less than 12 years old.
2. The bear is more than 9 years old.
3. The bear is not 11 years old.

How old is the bear that visits the pond?

MATERIALS

dark-colored counters (at least 19 per group); light-colored counters (at least 11 per group)

Understanding the Problem

- What did Keiko see in the mud near the pond? (*bear claw prints*)
- How many things did the ranger tell Keiko about the bear's age? (*3*)
- Is the bear 12 years old? (*no, he is younger than 12*)
- What numbers would show that he is younger than 12? (*1–11*)
- Is the bear 9 years old? (*no, he is older than 9*)
- Is the bear 11 years old? (*no*)

Solving the Problem

Use Logical Reasoning

- Can you find any numbers that are not the bear's age by using the clues?
- Can the bear be 12? (*no*) Why? (*the ranger said the bear was younger than 12*)
- Can he be 14? (*no, he is younger than 12*)
- Can he be 9? (*the ranger said the bear is older than 9*)
- Can he be 11? (*the ranger said the bear is not 11*)

Use Manipulatives

- Place light counters over the numbers that are possible after reading each clue.

- Place dark counters over the numbers that can't be correct answers.
- What age can the bear be? (*10*)

Solution

The bear is less than 12, so 12 through 20 is eliminated.

The bear is more than 9 years old, so 0–9 is eliminated.

The bear is not 11, so 10 is the only number left.

STRATEGY ASSESSMENT IDEAS

Listen and watch as students work to see if they

- use a plan to record their work
- correctly use all conditions given in the problem
- arrive at correct conclusions through reasoning

Related Problems: 47, 44, 43, 31, 24

Problem Extension

Figure out how old Keiko is! He is less than 12 years old and more than 9 years old. The ones digit of his age is 0. How old is Keiko? (*10 years old*)

SET 13

The Animal Shelter

Sam and Ellie woke up on Saturday morning bursting with excitement. "Is today the day?" asked Ellie. "Yes," said Sam. "Today is the day we get our new puppy from the animal shelter!"

Sam and Ellie had been living in an apartment in the city with their parents. Only one week ago they had moved into their new house in the country. They had been waiting for months for this special day to arrive.

The children were so excited they could hardly eat their breakfast. "Ellie, eat your cereal!" said her mother. "As soon as you're done we can leave." With this in mind, Ellie cleaned her bowl very quickly. Then they were ready to go. The drive to the animal shelter seemed to take forever. "Are we almost there? How much longer?" asked Sam.

At last they arrived at the shelter. They could hear the dogs barking. Each dog seemed to be saying, "Take me home with you." There were cages and cages of dogs and puppies. There were dogs of every kind and color. In a different part of the shelter there were cats and kittens.

Sam and Ellie walked very slowly past each cage. They wanted to be sure that they saw every dog and puppy. Suddenly Sam stopped. He pointed to a small beagle with sad brown eyes. "Look, Ellie," Sam said. They both went over to the little beagle's cage. Sam held out his hand very slowly, and said, "Hi, little puppy." The little beagle put his paw through the cage into Sam's hand. Sam and Ellie knew this was the special dog they had been looking for.

Discussion Questions

1. What is an animal shelter?
2. Why do you think Sam and Ellie had to wait to get their new puppy?
3. Did the shelter have only dogs and puppies? (*no*)
4. What did the little beagle do when Sam held out this hand? (*put its paw through the cage*)
5. What do you think would have happened if the beagle hadn't put his paw in Sam's hand?
6. Have you ever been to an animal shelter?

49 SKILL ACTIVITY

Tell a Subtraction Question for a Picture

Picture A

Discuss all features of the top picture on Blackline Master 41.

Possible Question for Picture A

How many more puppies are playing than are sleeping? (2)

Picture B

Discuss all features of the bottom picture on Blackline Master 41.

Possible Questions for Picture B

How many more puppies than kittens are eating? (3)

TEACHING ACTIONS

1. Show and discuss Picture A.
2. Ask students to tell a question that can be answered using subtraction.
3. Repeat for Picture B.
4. (*optional*) Have students answer their questions.

50 ONE-STEP PROBLEM

Sam and Ellie's new puppy had a big appetite. It seemed as though he was always hungry. On Friday Sam fed the puppy 8 times. On Saturday Ellie fed the puppy 11 times. How many more times did Ellie feed the puppy than Sam?

Understanding the Problem

- What does it mean to have a big appetite?
- Who fed the puppy on Friday? (*Sam*)
- When did Ellie feed the puppy? (*on Saturday*)
- How many times did Sam feed the puppy? (*8*)
- How many times did Ellie feed the puppy? (*11*)
- What do we want to find? (*how many more times Ellie fed the puppy than Sam*)

Solving the Problem

- Are you trying to find how many times the puppy was fed on the two days? (*no*)
- Which is more, 8 or 11? (*11*) How much more? (*3 more*)
- Can you draw a picture to show how many times the puppy was fed on each day? Does your picture help you answer the question?

Solution

Choose the Operation

11 − 8 = 3   or   11
                    − 8
                    ———
                      3

Ellie fed the puppy 3 more times than Sam.

Draw a Picture

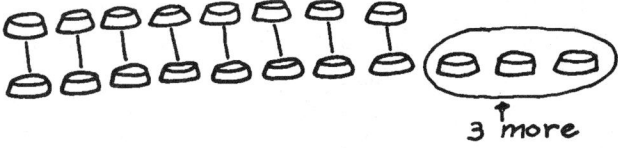

Related Problems: 46, 38, 30, 26

Problem Extensions

1. Suppose the puppy ate 11 times on Saturday. He ate 5 times on Saturday morning. How many times did he eat on the rest of Saturday? (*6 times*)
2. While Sam and Ellie were playing out in a field beside their house, they saw 9 baby rabbits and 13 baby squirrels. How many more baby squirrels did they see than baby rabbits? (*4 more*)

51 ▷ PROCESS PROBLEM

While Ellie and Sam were at the animal shelter, they saw 3 dogs wearing name tags and 1 dog without a name tag. The dog without a name tag was called Rollie. The dog with floppy ears was named Cleo. The dog with hair over its eyes was named Benji. And the smallest dog of all was Teeny. Can you decide which dog was called Rollie?

MATERIALS

square, trapezoid, triangle, and hexagon pattern blocks (1 of each shape per group)

Understanding the Problem

- How many dogs did Sam and Ellie see with name tags? (*3*)
- How many dogs did they see that were not wearing name tags? (*1*)
- What was the dog's name who was not wearing a name tag? (*Rollie*)
- What was the name of the dog with floppy ears? (*Cleo*)
- What was special about Benji? (*he had hair covering his eyes*)
- Who was the smallest dog? (*Teeny*)

Solving the Problem

Draw or Use a Picture/Use Logical Reasoning

- Which dog has floppy ears? (*Cleo*) Can you draw her name tag on her?
- Can you draw the name tag on the dog named Benji?
- Which dog is the smallest? (*Teeny*) Draw a name tag on her.
- Are there any dogs left without name tags? (*Yes*) What is his name? (*Rollie*)

Use Manipulatives

- Place the pattern blocks on the corresponding name tag. Try to match the tags to the pictures.
- Listen to the story a second time to check to see if the matches you made are correct.

Solution

 Cleo has floppy ears  Benji has hair over his eyes  Teeny is the smallest  This must be Rollie

Related Problems: 48, 47, 44, 43, 31

Problem Extension

Ellie saw 4 kittens playing with a ball of yarn. The kitten who was all white was called Fluffy. The kitten with stripes was called Taco. Lulu had two big spots. The other kitten's name was Midnight. Can you decide which kitten was Midnight? Why was he called Midnight? *Note:* Draw cats as described on the board or paper. Let students match names with cats.

STRATEGY ASSESSMENT IDEAS

Listen and watch as students work to see if they

- use a plan to place the blocks on the pictures
- correctly use all conditions given in the problem
- arrive at correct conclusions through reasoning

52 PROCESS PROBLEM

The animal shelter held a Shaggy Dog Contest. The dog with the longest, thickest coat of hair was named the winner. The prize was a big bone. Four shaggy dogs named Shadow, Ollie, Manfred, and Scout were in the contest. Scout came in last. Shadow finished between Scout and Manfred. Ollie was shaggier than Manfred. Who was the shaggiest dog?

MATERIALS

paper strips or crayons (4 of different lengths per group)

Understanding the Problem

- What is a shaggy dog? (*one that has a long, thick coat*)
- What prize did the shaggiest dog get? (*a big bone*)
- Who came in last place? (*Scout*)
- Who was shaggier, Ollie or Manfred? (*Ollie*)
- Where did Shadow finish? (*between Manfred and Scout*)
- Who was shaggier, Scout or Shadow? (*Shadow*)
- Are we trying to find out who won the bone? (*yes*)

Solving the Problem

Use Logical Reasoning/Use a Picture

- Who came in last? (*Scout*) Can you put his name where it belongs in the picture?
- Was Shadow shaggier than Scout? (*yes*) Was Shadow shaggier than Manfred? (*no*) Where does Shadow's name go?
- Was Manfred shaggier than Shadow? (*yes*) Was Manfred shaggier than Ollie? (*no*) Where does Manfred's name go?
- Who won? (*Ollie*) Put his name in the winner's place.

Use Manipulatives

- Use the 4 different strips of paper (or crayons) to show the length of the dogs' hair (long strip = long hair). Place the correct strip on each dog's name tag as you hear the clues.
- Which strip represents Scout? (*shortest*) Can Shadow be the winner? (*no*) Which strip represents Shadow? (*the next to the shortest*) Check your work, and record the dogs' names.

▶ *turn the page*

STRATEGY ASSESSMENT IDEAS

Listen and watch as students work to see if they

- use a plan to arrange the strips in order
- correctly use all conditions given in the problem
- arrive at correct conclusions through reasoning

Solution

Ollie was the shaggiest dog.

Related Problems: 51, 48, 47, 44, 43

Problem Extension

Cisco is the oldest kitten in the animal shelter. She is more than 12 weeks old but less than 15 weeks old. If you count by 2s, you will soon reach her age. How old is Cisco? (*14 weeks old*)

SET 14

Learning to Ice Skate

Sunday morning dawned frosty and bright. There was a fresh layer of snow on the ground. Ben thought sadly to himself, "This is a perfect day for ice skating, unfortunately." Ben's Uncle Ted lived on a lake, and he had invited Ben and his sister, Jill, to come ice skating. But Ben was nervous about skating. He had tried skating once the winter before and had fallen down more times than he liked to remember. Jill was a good skater. That made things even worse.

Uncle Ted didn't live very far away. Ben, Jill, and their mother arrived at his house shortly before noon. There was a cheery fire burning in the fireplace. Ben wanted to stay inside where it was warm, but his mother, Uncle Ted, and Jill were already putting on extra socks and sweaters. Ben tried to think of an excuse to keep from going skating and falling down all afternoon.

"Mom, I think I'll stay inside and do my homework," he said. Ben was sure that would work on his mother. She always wanted him to do his homework.

"Ben," said his mother, "don't be silly. We're here to skate!"

The best excuse in the world had failed. So Ben put on his skates and stood up. He moved his right foot forward. Amazing! He was still standing. Then he moved his left foot. Slowly—very slowly—he began to move on the ice.

"I'm skating, I'm . . . whoa . . ." Oh no! He had fallen down already. Uncle Ted skated over swiftly. He helped Ben up. He began giving Ben some pointers on ice skating. Ben tried again. This time he stayed up a little longer. It was beginning to be kind of fun. He thought, "Maybe skating isn't so bad after all."

Discussion Questions

1. Why didn't Ben want to go skating? (*he had fallen down too many times before*)
2. Did Ben's sister Jill skate well? (*yes*)
3. What excuse did Ben use to try to keep from skating? (*that he had to do homework*)
4. What do you think would have happened if Ben had kept falling down?
5. Have you ever been ice skating? Would it be fun?

53 ▶ SKILL ACTIVITY

Tell Why an Answer Is Not Reasonable

Problem A
When Ben and Jill left to go skating, it was 14 degrees outside. When they got home after skating, they looked at the thermometer—it was now only 8 degrees outside. By how many degrees had the temperature changed?

Unreasonable Answer to Problem A
22 degrees

Problem B
Ben and Jill live 11 kilometers from their grandparents' house. When they go to visit their grandparents, they pass by the lake where they go skating in the winter. The lake is 6 kilometers from where Ben and Jill live. How far is it from the lake to their grandparents' house?

Unreasonable Answer to Problem B
6 kilometers

Note: One way to keep students from solving the problems right away is to tell them that they should not have pencil in their hands.

TEACHING ACTIONS

1. Read Problem A to the students. (Do not ask them to solve it.)
2. Tell them the "unreasonable" answer.
3. Have students tell why the answer is not reasonable. (Phrasing might be: "Do you think ____ is a reasonable answer? Why?" or "Do you think ____ is a good answer? Why?")
4. Repeat for Problem B.
5. (*optional*) Have students solve each problem.

54 ONE-STEP PROBLEM

The first day Ben went skating, he fell down 11 times. The second day he went skating, he fell down only 7 times. How many times did Ben fall down the 2 days he went skating?

Understanding the Problem

- How many times did Ben fall down the first day he went skating? (*11 times*)
- How many times did he fall down the second day? (*7 times*)
- Why did Ben fall down so many times? (*he was just learning how to skate*)
- Are we trying to find out which day he fell down more? (*no, we want to find how many times in all*)

Solving the Problem

- Can you write a number sentence for this story? (*see solution*)
- Is this an addition story or a subtraction story? (*addition*)
- If Ben fell down 2 times the first day and 1 time the second day, how many times did he fall down in the two days? (*3 times*) Can you use the same operation to solve the problem for 11 times and 7 times?

Solution

Choose the Operation

$11 + 7 = 18$ or $\begin{array}{r} 11 \\ + 7 \\ \hline 18 \end{array}$

Ben fell down 18 times in the 2 days.

Related Problems: 42, 34, 22, 18

Problem Extension

Jill is a pretty good skater. The first day she went skating she fell down 5 times, the second day only 3 times, and the third day 3 times. How many times did she fall down on the 3 days? (*11 times*)

55 ▶ PROCESS PROBLEM

Uncle Ted wanted to see how long Ben and Jill could skate without falling down. He marked off 6 different courses for them to follow. Each course started at the same place and finished at the same place, but the paths the courses took were different. Can you list the 6 different courses to go from start to finish?

Understanding the Problem

- What did Uncle Ted want to find out? (*how long Ben and Jill could skate without falling down*)
- How many different courses did he mark off? (*6*)
- What is a course? (*a path to follow from START to FINISH*)
- Did each course start at a different place? (*no, all courses started at the same place*)
- Did each course finish at the same place? (*yes*)
- How many paths can the children take when they start? (*2*)
- How many paths can they take to reach the flag? (*2*) What are the numbers of these paths? (*1 and 2*)
- How may paths can they take from the flag to the finish? (*3*) What are the numbers of these paths? (*3, 4, and 5*)

Solving the Problem

- If Ben took path 1 first, which path could he take when he reached the flag? (*3, 4, or 5*) Can you write down one path Ben could take? Now write down the other paths.
- If Ben took path 1 first, couldn't he take path 3, 4, or 5 to reach the finish? Write these paths down. (refer to bottom of Blackline Master 45)
- If Ben took path 2 first, what paths could he take after he reached the flag? (*3, 4, or 5*) Write the paths down. (refer to bottom of Blackline Master 45)

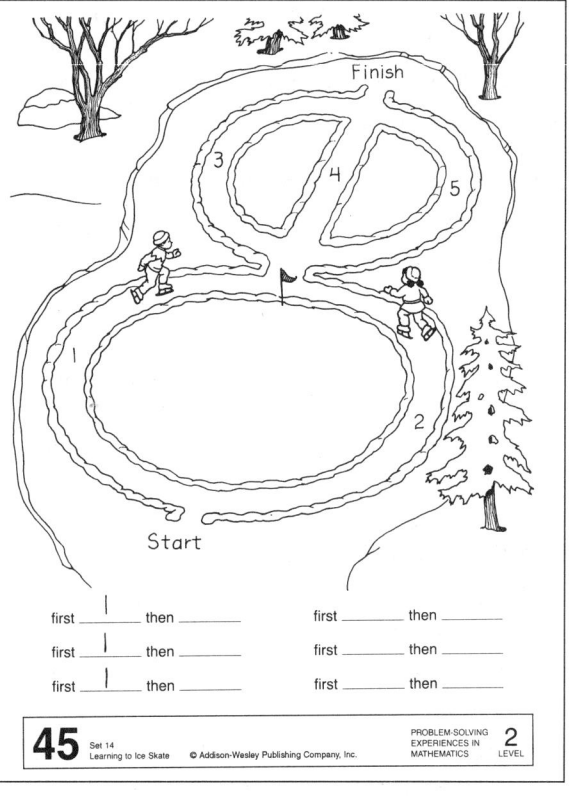

Solution

Complete an Organized List

First 1 then 3   First 2 then 3
First 1 then 4   First 2 then 4
First 1 then 5   First 2 then 5

Related Problems: 28, 27, 7, 4, 3

Problem Extension

Suppose there were 3 paths from the start to the flag and 3 paths from the flag to the finish. (Have students draw another path on their papers.) How many different trips could Jill and Ben take from START to FINISH? (*9 in all*)

STRATEGY ASSESSMENT IDEAS

Listen and watch as students work to see if they

- create correct entries for their lists
- organize entries in their lists
- list all possibilities

56 PROCESS PROBLEM

Ben, Jill, and two of their friends—Sarah and John—like to skate. The table shows how many times Ben, Jill, Sarah, and John went skating during the winter. Which 3 children went skating 23 times in all?

MATERIALS

counters (23 per group)

Understanding the Problem

- What does the table tell us? (*how many times each of the 4 children went skating*)
- How many times did Ben go skating? (*7*)
- Who went skating 8 times? (*John*)
- Who sent skating the most? (*Sarah*)
- What are we trying to find out about the 4 children? (*which 3 went skating a total of 23 times*)

Solving the Problem

Guess and Check

- How many times did Ben, Jill, and Sarah go skating? (*22*) Is this the answer we're looking for? (*no*) Is it too low or too high? (*too low*)
- Which 3 children went skating the most? (*Ben, Sarah, and John*) How many times did they go skating? (*24 times*) Is this the answer we're looking for? (*no*) Is it too low or too high? (*too high*)
- If one number is 9, what must the other numbers be to make 23 in all? (*14*) What 2 numbers add up to 14? (*6 and 8*)
- If 2 of the numbers are 6 and 8, what must the other number be to make 23 in all? (*9*)

Use Manipulatives

- Each person in your group will represent one of the children from the story. Take the number of counters that tells how many times your person went skating.
- Take turns combining the counters from the other 3 members of your group.
- Record this information to tell you which 3 children went skating a total of 23 times.

STRATEGY ASSESSMENT IDEAS

Listen and watch as students work to see if they

- make a reasonable first guess (students should use only 3 numbers listed in the table)
- make a second guess using what they learn from checking the first guess
- check their work to make sure they used all the information

Ben	Jill	Sarah	John
7	6	9	8

Solution

- Try 7 + 6 + 9 = 22 (*too low*)
- Try 7 + 9 + 8 = 21 (*too high*)
- Try 6 + 9 + 8 = 23 (*correct*)

Jill, Sarah, and John went skating 23 times.

Related Problems: 52, 51, 48, 47, 44

Problem Extension

(Use the same table.) Which 2 children went skating a total of 15 times? (*2 solutions: Ben and John; Jill and Sarah*)

Note: If a student gets one solution only, ask, "Is that the only one?"

SET 15

Pony Rides

Kirsten, José, and Mary Beth could not believe their good luck. After several months of begging and pleading with their parents, they were finally going to go to their grandfather's pony farm. They were going to drive to his farm that very day!

It took them 3 hours to drive there, but finally they were rounding the last curve and the farm was in sight. "Granddaddy, Granddaddy!" shouted Mary Beth. "We've come to ride your ponies!"

Kirsten and José were out of the car and down to the barn within seconds. Mary Beth came running after them, and their grandfather followed closely behind. "This is the one I want to ride!" shouted José. He pointed to a beautiful black-and-white pony.

"Yes, she is a pretty pinto," said grandfather. "Would you all like a chance to ride her?"

"Yes. Yes!" Kirsten, José, and Mary Beth all cried at once. They spent the rest of the day riding the pretty black-and-white pony, and what a happy day it was!

Discussion Questions

1. Why were Kirsten, José, and Mary Beth so lucky? (*they got to go to their grandfather's pony farm*)
2. How old do you think the children are?
3. What did the pony that José chose look like? (*it was black and white*)
4. Did all the children ride different ponies? (*no*)
5. Have you ever ridden on a pony?

57 SKILL ACTIVITY

Complete a Picture to Show a Story

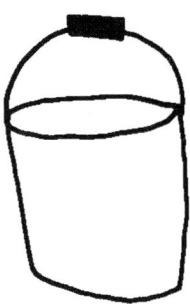 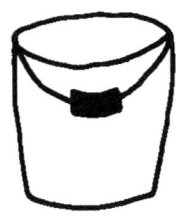

Story

Each day Grandfather gives his black-and-white pony 2 buckets of oats to eat. Grandfather has 7 ponies in all, and each pony eats 2 buckets of oats every day.

TEACHING ACTIONS

1. Draw a picture of 2 buckets on the board (as shown) and have students copy it. Tell them, "These are 2 buckets of oats for 1 pony for 1 day."
2. Read the story to the students. Have them draw the buckets for the other ponies.
3. Show different students' pictures.
4. *(optional)* Ask students to find out how many buckets of oats the 7 ponies eat.

58 ONE-STEP PROBLEM

Kirsten, José, and Mary Beth were at their grandfather's pony farm for 2 days. Kirsten and José each took 12 pony rides during the 2 days. Mary Beth took 6 pony rides on day 1 and 7 pony rides on day 2. How many pony rides did Mary Beth take during the 2 days?

Understanding the Problem

- How many days were Kirsten, José, and Mary Beth at the pony farm? (*2 days*)
- Did José take 12 pony rides? (*yes*)
- How many pony rides did Mary Beth take on the first day? (*6*) The second day? (*7*)
- Are we trying to find out on which day Mary Beth took more rides? (*no, how many rides in 2 days*)

Solving the Problem

- If Mary Beth took 1 ride on day 1 and 2 rides on day 2, how many rides did she take in the 2 days? (*3*) Now can you do the problem?
- Can you write a number sentence for this problem? (*see solution*)
- Are you being asked to put together the rides on 2 days? (*yes*) Which operation involves putting together? (*addition*)

Solution

Choose the Operation

$6 + 7 = 13$ or $\begin{array}{r} 6 \\ + 7 \\ \hline 13 \end{array}$

Mary Beth took 13 rides on the 2 days.

Related Problems: 54, 42, 34, 22, 18

Problem Extensions

1. Mary Beth took 7 pony rides on the second day and José took 5 pony rides on the second day. How many rides did Mary Beth and José take on the second day? (*12 rides*)

2. Mary Beth took 6 pony rides on day 1, José took 7 rides, and Kirsten took 4 rides. How many rides did all 3 children take on day 1? (*17 rides*)

Note: This is a 2-step problem; that is, 2 additions are required.

59 PROCESS PROBLEM

On Saturdays, children from all around come to the pony farm to ride the ponies. It costs 3¢ for each ride. If you were to take 7 rides, how much would it cost you?

MATERIALS

pennies or counters (at least 21 per pair)

Understanding the Problem

- Why do children come to the pony farm on Saturdays? (*for pony rides*)
- How much does it cost for a ride? (*3¢*)
- What do we want to know about the pony rides? (*how much 7 rides cost*)

Solving the Problem

Complete a Table/Look for a Pattern

- Look at the table. If each ride costs 3¢, how much do 2 rides cost? (*6¢*) 3 rides? (*9¢*)
- How much more do 2 rides cost than 1 ride? (*3¢*) How much more do 3 rides cost than 2 rides? (*3¢*)
- How much do 4 rides cost? (*12¢*) 5 rides? (*15¢*)
- Can you start with a 3 and count by 3s? When would you stop? (*at 21*)

Use Manipulatives

- Instruct students to form piles of pennies that contain 3 pennies each.
- How many pony rides do you get for 1 pile of pennies? (*1*)
- How many piles would it take to ride 2 times? (*2*)
- How many pennies would it take to ride 2 times? (*6*)
- How many piles would it take to ride 3 times? (*3*)
- How many pennies would it take to ride 3 times? (*9*)
- Do you see a pattern that can help you complete the rest of the table? (*each ride costs 1 more pile of pennies, an increase of 3¢*)

Solution

Number of Rides	1	2	3	4	5	6	7
Cost	3¢	6¢	9¢	12¢	15¢	18¢	21¢

7 rides cost 21¢.

Related Problems: 40, 39, 36, 35, 16

Problem Extension

Lois has 28¢. How many rides can she take? Use the table. (*she can take 9 rides and have 1¢ left*)

STRATEGY ASSESSMENT IDEAS

Listen and watch as students work to see if they

- correctly place pennies into piles of 3
- use a pattern to correctly extend the table
- interpret the table to arrive at the correct answer

60 PROCESS PROBLEM

Each pony on the farm wears a blanket under its saddle. The blankets are red, blue, or yellow. Deanna, the ponies' groomer, is lining the ponies up for a picture. There are 9 ponies in all. Deanna lined up 4 of the ponies and told the children she had made a pattern with the blankets. She then added 2 more ponies to the line up and asked the children to tell her which pony should line up next. *Note:* Have students color the blankets on horses 1–6 in the order red, blue, blue, yellow, red, blue.

MATERIALS

red, yellow, and blue interlocking cubes (at least 4 of each color per group); red, yellow, and blue crayons or markers

Understanding the Problem

- What colors were the ponies' blankets on the pony farm? (*red, yellow, and blue*)
- How many ponies are there? (*9*)
- Why did Deanna line them up one day? (*to have their pictures taken*)
- How many ponies did Deanna put in a line? (*6*)
- How many ponies did the children add to the pattern? (*3*)

Solving the Problem

Look for a Pattern

- What color blanket comes after red? (*blue*)
- What color blanket comes after yellow? (*red*)
- What color comes next—red, blue, or yellow? (*blue*)
- If 2 blue blankets are lined up next to each other, what blanket comes next? (*yellow*)
- What color blanket is seventh? (*blue*) What color blanket should line up after the blue blanket? (*yellow*) What color lines up last? (*red*)

Use Manipulatives

- Instruct students to "saddle up" (place a cube on the pony's back) the ponies according to the colors indicated.

STRATEGY ASSESSMENT IDEAS

Listen and watch as students work to see if they

- describe the pattern formed by the ponies
- extend the pattern correctly
- use the pattern to arrive at the correct answer

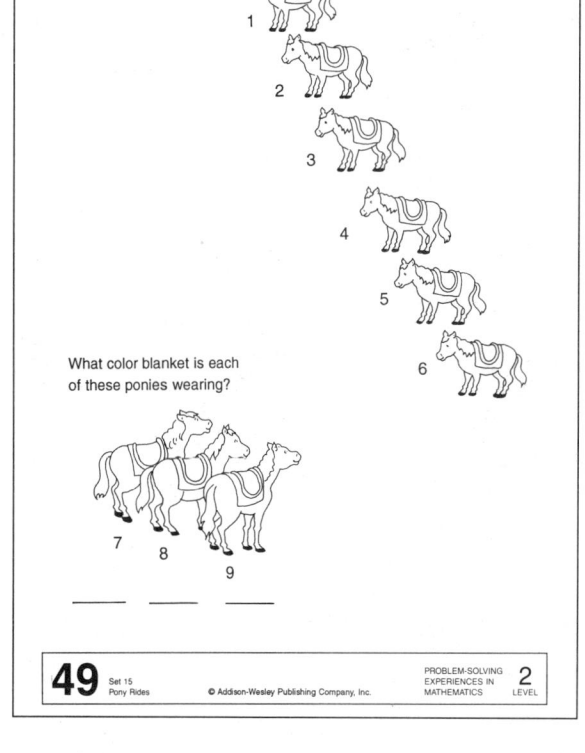

Solution

Look for a Pattern

Pattern: red, blue, blue, yellow, red, blue, blue, yellow, red

The last 3 ponies are wearing blue, yellow, and red blankets in that order.

Related Problems: 59, 40, 39, 36, 35

Problem Extension

If there were 12 ponies in all, in what order would the next 3 line up? (*blue, blue, yellow*) What color would the eighth pony be? (*yellow*) The tenth? (*blue*) The twelfth? (*yellow*)

Note: This extension also reviews the students' understanding of ordinal numbers.

SET 16

A Special Pig

Tai lived on a farm. Tai liked to draw the animals that lived on his farm. He especially liked to draw the pigs. Sometimes, Tai would make up stories using his drawings. Here is one of Tai's stories.

Max the pig was a special pig. He could talk. He could also play the guitar. Today was a special day for Max. Today was his birthday! He wasn't sure, but he thought the other pigs in the barnyard were planning a surprise birthday party for him.

When Max walked into the barn, the other pigs were whispering. As soon as they saw him, they stopped whispering. Max asked, "What were you talking about?" The other pigs said they were just discussing the spring picnic. "Oh," said Max. He was disappointed. He thought for sure they had been planning his birthday party.

Max decided to play the guitar to make himself feel better. He played "Piggy Went a Courtin'." He played many other of his favorite songs. When he was finished, he slowly walked back to the barn. As he walked around the corner, SURPRISE! All of the other pigs were there. They had baked a huge birthday cake for him!

"I thought no one had remembered by birthday!" exclaimed Max. "Well," said one of the other pigs, "we were whispering so you wouldn't hear us planning your birthday party. It was supposed to be a big surprise."

Max was so happy that he turned a somersault in the air.

After Tai had finished writing his story and coloring his drawings, he tacked it to a wall in the barn. Tai's family enjoyed reading his story! They want Tai to write another story about the horses on the farm.

Discussion Questions

1. Where does Tai live? (*on a farm*)
2. What does he like to do? (*draw the farm animals and write stories*)
3. Could Max the pig really talk? (*no*)
4. Why were the pigs in Tai's story whispering? (*they were planning a surprise party*)
5. Where did Tai put his story and drawings after he was finished? (*on a wall in the barn*)
6. What animal would you like to write a story about?

61 ▷ SKILL ACTIVITY

Tell the Operation for a Story Problem

Problem A
There are large pigs and small pigs on Tai's farm. How many of each kind of pig are on the farm?

Numbers: 8 large pigs, 5 small pigs

Problem B
Tai has several chickens but only a few horses. How many more chickens does Tai have than horses?

Numbers: 7 chickens, 3 horses

Notes: The focus of this activity is on choosing the operation to solve a problem, not on solving the problem. Addition is used when sets of objects are joined or put together; subtraction is used whenever

1. sets are compared
2. sets are separated (taken apart)
3. objects are added to a set to get a desired number

The 3 subtraction types are, respectively, comparison, take away, and missing addend.

TEACHING ACTIONS

1. Read and discuss Problem A.
2. Ask students: "If we knew how many large and how many small pigs are on Tai's farm, what operation (addition or subtraction) would we use to answer the question?" (Give students numbers.)
3. Point out that when the problem involves joining or putting together 2 groups, we use addition to find how many in both groups together.
4. Read and discuss Problem B.
5. Ask students: "If we knew how many chickens and how many horses Tai has, would we add or subtract to answer the question?" (Give students numbers.)
6. Point out that when we compare 2 groups, we subtract to find which has more.

62 ONE-STEP PROBLEM

Ms. Shaw, a farmer, planted 34 rows of carrots. One morning when she went to water her carrots, she found that rabbits had eaten the green tops off all the carrots in 13 rows. How many rows of carrots were not eaten by the rabbits?

Understanding the Problem

- What did Ms. Shaw plant? (*carrots or rows of carrots*)
- How many rows of carrots did she plant? (*34*)
- What did she find one morning? (*rabbits had eaten the tops off some of the carrots*)
- How many rows of carrot tops did the rabbits eat? (*13*)
- What is a row? (*a straight line; in this story, a line of carrots*)

Solving the Problem

- Does this story involve joining groups together? (*no*) Does it involve taking away part of something? (*yes*)
- What operation, addition or subtraction, should you use? (*subtraction*)
- Can you write a subtraction sentence for this problem? (*see solution*)
- Can you draw 34 rows of carrots and mark out 13 rows?

Solution

Choose the Operation

34 − 13 = 21   or   34
                      − 13
                      ────
                        21

21 rows of carrots were not eaten.

Draw a Picture

21 rows were not eaten by rabbits.

Related Problems: 50, 46, 38, 30, 26

Problem Extensions

1. Ms. Shaw planted 34 rows of carrots and 23 rows of corn. How many more rows of carrots did she plant than corn? (*comparison type of subtraction; 11 rows*)
2. Ms. Shaw planted 16 potato plants. A pig dug up 7 of the plants. How many of the plants were not dug up? (*take-away type of subtraction; 9 plants*)

63 ▶ PROCESS PROBLEM

Tai drew 3 baby brothers for Max, one of his pigs. Baby pigs are called piglets. Tai named the piglets Porky, Paul, and Pete. Of course, Max is the biggest. Pete is bigger than Porky but smaller than Paul. Can you match each drawing of a pig with his name? (Read names shown on Blackline Master 51 to the students.)

MATERIALS

paper strips or crayons (at least 4 of different lengths per group)

Understanding the Problem

- How many baby pigs did Tai draw? (3)
- What is a baby pig called? (*piglet*)
- What are the piglets' names? (*Porky, Paul, and Pete*)
- Of the 4 pigs, which pig is the biggest? (*Max*)
- Is Pete bigger than Max? (*no*)
- Is Pete bigger than Porky? (*yes*)
- Who is bigger, Pete or Paul? (*Paul*)

Solving the Problem

Use Logical Reasoning

- Can you draw a line from Max to his name?
- Is Porky smaller than Pete? (*yes*) Is Porky smaller than Paul? (*yes*) Can you draw a line to show which drawing is Porky?
- How many pigs are left? (*2*) Who is bigger, Paul or Pete? (*Paul*) Can you draw lines to show which is Paul and which is Pete?

Use Manipulatives

- Of the 4 pigs, which is the biggest? (*Max*) Measure the pigs' heights with your paper strips. Find Max.
- Do some more measuring. Measure the other 3 pigs.
- Which pig is Pete? (Remember, Pete is bigger than Porky and smaller than Paul.)

STRATEGY ASSESSMENT IDEAS

Listen and watch as students work to see if they

- use a plan to arrange the strips
- correctly use all conditions given in the problem
- arrive at correct conclusions through reasoning

Solution

Use Logical Reasoning

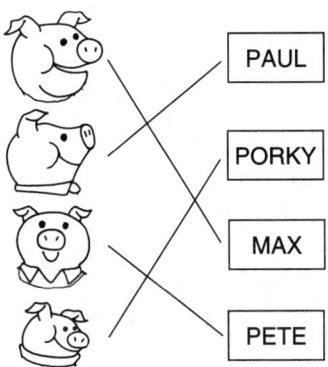

Pigs in order of size: Max is the largest, then Paul, Pete, and Porky.

Related Problems: 56, 52, 51, 48, 47

Problem Extension

Tai makes other cartoons using the 3 piglets. Each piglet plays a different instrument. Use the clues to decide which piglet plays which instrument. Clues: You blow into Paul's instrument to make music. Pete's instrument is large and has keys. You have to find out Porky's instrument.

Note: Draw a guitar, horn, piano, and drum on the board. Let students match names to instruments. Max—guitar, Paul—horn, Pete—piano, Porky—drum.

64 PROCESS PROBLEM

Ms. Shaw, the farmer, made 5 scarecrows to put in her fields. Scarecrows are used to scare away crows and other birds from eating corn and other crops growing in the fields. After looking over the scarecrows, Tai decided on one that was the scariest of all. To find which scarecrow Tai thought was the scariest, look at the pictures and use the clues.

Understanding the Problem

- What did Ms. Shaw make? (*scarecrows*)
- What is a scarecrow? (*a dummy dressed up to scare birds away from crops*)
- How many scarecrows did she make? (*5*)
- What are crops? (*plants like corn, beans, and carrots that farmers plant*)
- Did Tai decide on one that was the scariest of all? (*yes*)

Solving the Problem

- Can you draw a ring around the scarecrows that have brooms?
- Can you draw a ring around the scarecrows that are wearing coats?
- Can you draw a ring around the scarecrows that are wearing scarves?
- Which scarecrow has 3 rings around it?

Solution

Use Logical Reasoning

Clue 1 eliminates two of the scarecrows, leaving scarecrows 1, 3, and 4.

Clue 2 eliminates scarecrow 1, leaving 3 and 4.

Clue 3 eliminates scarecrow 3, leaving 4.

Tai thought scarecrow 4 was the scariest.

Related Problems: 63, 56, 52, 51, 48

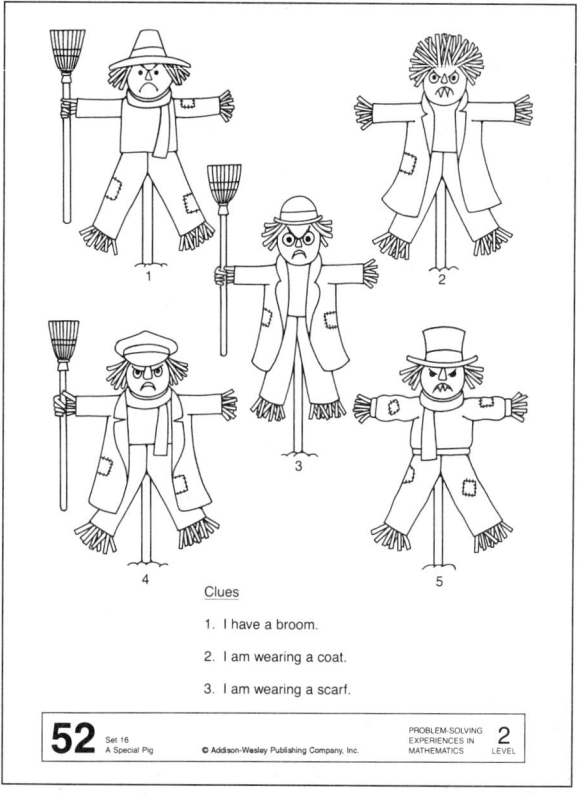

Problem Extensions

1. Give the following clues to accompany the original pictures of scarecrows.
   a. I am wearing a scarf.
   b. I do not have on a coat.
   c. I do not have a broom. (*scarecrow 5*)
2. Give these clues to accompany the original pictures of scarecrows.
   a. I am wearing a coat.
   b. I am not wearing a scarf.
   c. I do not have a broom. (*scarecrow 2*)

STRATEGY ASSESSMENT IDEAS

Listen and watch as students work to see if they

- use a plan to record their work
- correctly use all conditions given in the problem
- arrive at correct conclusions through reasoning

Room 7

Ms. Nomura teaches second grade in Room 7 at Oakdale Elementary School. Every student in Room 7 gets to do at least 2 jobs each day. They each do one job in the morning and one job in the afternoon just before it's time to go home. Ms. Nomura has a large chart on the wall with cards that are hung on hooks. Each card has a different job written on it. As soon as school starts in the morning, Ms. Nomura has each student pick one morning job card and one afternoon job card.

Some days there are special jobs that need to be done. Ms. Nomura has a box on her desk with each student's name written on a piece of paper. When she needs someone to do a special job, she covers her eyes and picks a piece of paper from the box. She reads the name on the paper, and that person gets to do the special job. Just yesterday, Ms. Nomura had a special job and I was picked to do it!

Discussion Questions

1. What grade does Ms. Nomura teach at Oakdale Elementary School? (*second grade*)
2. What does every student in Room 7 get to do each day? (*2 jobs*)
3. What types of jobs might the students have to do in the morning? The afternoon?
4. Why does Ms. Nomura cover her eyes when she picks a piece of paper with a student's name on it from the box?
5. Can you think of a special job Ms. Nomura might ask a student to do?

65 SKILL ACTIVITY

Tell the Operation

Problem A
There were 9 boys and 7 girls in Ms. Nomura's class on Monday. How many more boys than girls were in Ms. Nomura's class on Monday?

Problem B
On Ms. Nomura's bulletin board, there are __ jobs that need to be done in the morning and __ jobs that need to be done in the afternoon. What is the total number of jobs that need to be done in Room 7?

Problem C
Ms. Nomura told __ of the students to clean their desks. So far, only __ of them have done their job. How many more still have to clean their desk?

Note: Problem B is an addition situation. Problem C is a missing-addend subtraction situation.

TEACHING ACTIONS

1. Read Problem A. Have students tell the operation they would use to solve the problem. Do not have them solve it. Discuss their choice.

2. Tell students you are going to read another story, but now you are going to leave out the numbers. Read Problem B, and have students tell the operation they would use to solve it. Discuss why.

3. Repeat Teaching Action 2 for Problem C.

66 ONE-STEP PROBLEM

A soup company was giving away playground equipment to the school that collected the most soup labels in one month. In Room 7, Kyle's job was to count the soup labels brought in each day. On the first day of the contest, only 6 soup labels were brought in to Kyle. Ms. Nomura reminded all of the children about the contest and asked them to try to bring in more soup labels the next day. The next day, 14 soup labels were brought in to Kyle. How many more soup labels were brought in the second day than were brought in the first day?

Understanding the Problem

- How can a school get playground equipment from the soup company? (*by bringing in the most soup labels*)
- What was Kyle's job in Room 7? (*counting labels*)
- How many soup labels were brought in the first day? (*6*)
- What did Ms. Nomura remind the students of? (*to bring in soup labels*)
- How many soup labels was Kyle given on the second day? (*14*)
- What are we trying to find? (*how many more soup labels were brought in the second day than were brought in the first day*)

Solving the Problem

- Are you trying to find the total number of soup labels brought in? (*no*) So, do you use addition to solve this problem? (*no*)
- If you want to compare 2 numbers to find how much greater one is than the other, which operation should you use? (*subtraction*)

Solution

Choose the Operation

$$14 - 6 = 8 \quad \text{or} \quad \begin{array}{r} 14 \\ -6 \\ \hline 8 \end{array}$$

8 more soup labels were brought in the second day.

Related Problems: 62, 50, 46, 38, 30

Problem Extension

What is the total number of soup labels brought in for the first 2 days? (*20*)

67 PROCESS PROBLEM

In Room 7, every student has to choose one job to do in the morning and one job to do in the afternoon just before it's time to go home. When it was Heather's turn to choose, there were 3 morning jobs left for her to choose from and 2 afternoon jobs. Ms. Nomura told Heather that there are 6 different ways she could pick 1 morning job and 1 afternoon job. Can you find the 6 ways?

Understanding the Problem

- What does every student have to do in Room 7? (*a job in the morning and a job in the afternoon*)
- How many morning jobs did Heather have to choose from? (*3*) Afternoon jobs? (*2*)
- How many different ways can Heather choose 1 morning job and 1 afternoon job? (*6*)

Solving the Problem

- Pick one morning job. Write it on the tag at the bottom. Now, pick 1 afternoon job and write it with the morning job you picked. Can you find another way to do this?
- Suppose you choose to collect milk money in the morning. What is 1 afternoon job you can do with this? What is another afternoon job you can do with this?

Solution

Complete an Organized List

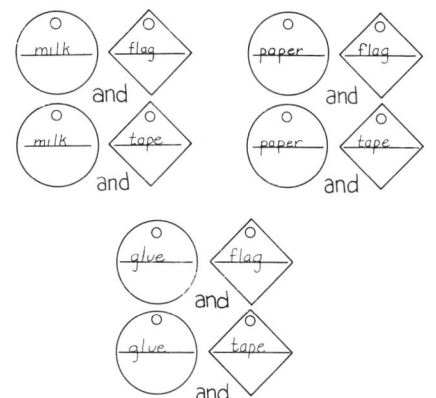

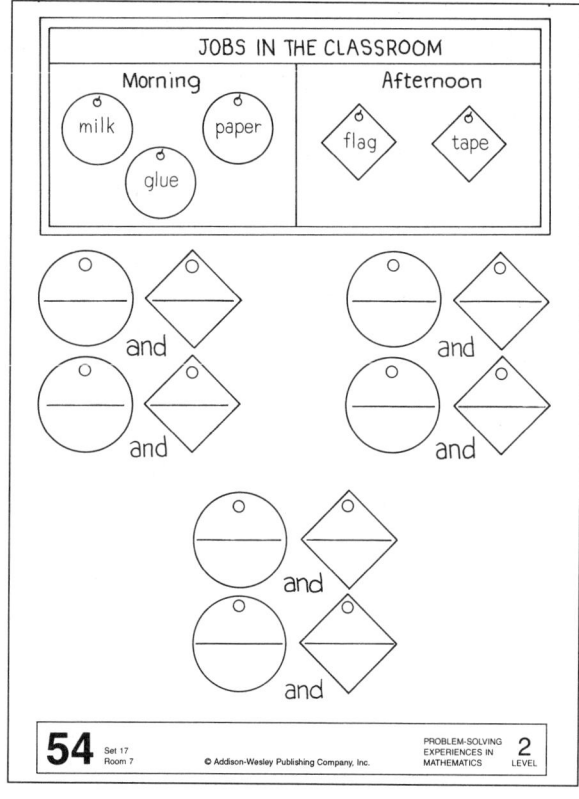

Related Problems: 55, 28, 27, 7, 4

Problem Extension

Suppose there were a third afternoon job of putting books away. Now how many choices would Heather have? (*3 more or 9 altogether*)

STRATEGY ASSESSMENT IDEAS

Listen and watch as students work to see if they

- create correct entries for their lists
- organize entries in their lists
- list all possibilities

68 PROCESS PROBLEM

Ms. Nomura has Room 7 divided into 5 reading groups. On Wednesday, the students in Room 7 were going to have their school pictures taken. On Tuesday, Ms. Nomura asked Rosa to choose which 3 reading groups would have their pictures taken in the morning and which 2 reading groups would have their pictures taken after lunch. Nine of the children in Ms. Nomura's class had their pictures taken in the morning. Which reading groups did Rosa choose to have their pictures taken in the morning?

MATERIALS

counters (9 per group)

Understanding the Problem

- How many reading groups does Ms. Nomura have Room 7 divided into? (*5*) Can you point to each group on your paper?
- How many students are in group 1? (*4*) 2? (*6*) 3? (*3*) 4? (*5*) 5? (*2*)
- Did all the groups have their pictures taken in the morning? (*no*) How many groups had their pictures taken in the morning? (*3*) How many children had their pictures taken in the morning? (*9*)
- What are we trying to find out about this class? (*which groups had their pictures taken in the morning*)

Solving the Problem

Guess and Check

- Could groups 2 and 3 be the only groups selected for the morning? (*no, 3 groups were selected*)
- Could groups 1, 3, and 4 be the ones selected? (*no, only 9 children were selected*)
- Which operation did you use to find the total number of children in the 3 groups? (*addition*)
- Can you guess which 3 groups were selected and add to check your guess?

Use Manipulatives

- Use your 9 counters and the drawing. Place a counter on each person who will have their picture taken before lunch.
- Place 1 counter on each member of a reading group. Choose a second reading group and place 1 counter on each member. Do you have exactly enough counters to cover all the members of a third reading group? Try other combinations.

▶ *turn the page*

STRATEGY ASSESSMENT IDEAS

Listen and watch as students work to see if they

- make a reasonable first guess (students should choose 3 different groups)
- make a second guess using what they learn from checking their first guess
- can use counters to check their guesses

Solution

Guess and Check

- Try groups 1, 2, and 3: 4 + 6 + 3 = 13 (*too high*)
- Try groups 3, 4, and 5: 3 + 5 + 2 = 10 (*too high*)
- Try groups 1, 3, and 5: 4 + 3 + 2 = 9 (*correct*)

Rosa picked groups 1, 3, and 5 to have their pictures taken in the morning.

Related Problems: 56, 32, 31, 8, 7

Problem Extension

Which 3 groups could go if the photographer said that 14 children could be photographed before lunch? (*groups 2, 3, and 4*)

The Imaginary Farm

Have you ever been to a farm? Most farms have chickens that look like chickens and act the way chickens are supposed to act, and most have cows that look like regular cows and do what cows are supposed to do. Most farms have different kinds of animals that look and act the way you would expect. But at the Imaginary Farm, the animals are not like regular animals. You see, this is not a real farm, it is made up of animals in your imagination.

At the Imaginary Farm, the animals look funny and they do funny things. Ralph, an old goat, wears an old hat and sneakers on all of his feet. Jenny, a chicken, always wears sunglasses and lies on top of the chicken house in a bathing suit. And Nel, a green cow, loves to play soccer. Maybe you can think of other animals that could live at the Imaginary Farm.

Discussion Questions

1. What kinds of animals might you see at a farm?
2. Do the animals at the Imaginary Farm dress and act like regular animals? (*no*)
3. Can you tell one of the funny animals you might see at the Imaginary Farm?
4. Suppose you saw a pig at the Imaginary Farm. How would the pig look funny and what kinds of funny things might the pig do?

69 SKILL ACTIVITY

Tell a Problem

Story A

The horses and cows played a soccer game on Saturday at the Imaginary Farm. There were 25 horses on one team. There were 13 cows on the other team.

Possible Questions for Story A

1. How many more horses than cows played soccer? *(12)*
2. Altogether, how many horses and cows played soccer? *(38)*

Story B

Horses at the Imaginary Farm don't wear regular horseshoes. Instead, they wear sneakers! They have 2 colors of sneakers, red and green. Last week, all of the horses' sneakers were washed. 46 red sneakers were washed and 32 green sneakers were washed.

Possible Questions for Story B

1. How many more red sneakers than green sneakers were washed? *(14)*
2. What is the total number of red and green sneakers that were washed? *(78)*

TEACHING ACTIONS

1. Read Story A to the students.
2. Have students tell questions they can answer using data from the story. Solicit a variety of questions.
3. *(optional)* Have students find the answers to the questions.
4. Repeat for Story B.

70 ONE-STEP PROBLEM

At the Imaginary Farm, sheep come in 2 colors, green and purple (not the usual colors of white and black!). There are 23 green sheep at the Imaginary Farm. There are 14 more purple sheep than green sheep. How many purple sheep are at the Imaginary Farm?

Understanding the Problem

- Do sheep at the Imaginary Farm come in the usual colors of black and white? (*no*) What colors are the sheep? (*green and purple*)
- How many green sheep are at the Imaginary Farm? (*23*)
- What do you know about the number of purple sheep at the Imaginary Farm? (*14 more purple sheep than green sheep*)
- What are we trying to find in this problem? (*how many purple sheep are at the Imaginary Farm*)

Solving the Problem

- Suppose your friend has 2¢. If you have 3 more pennies than your friend, how many pennies would you have? (*5*) Which operation did you use to find that answer? (*addition*)
- If there was one more purple sheep than green sheep, how many purple sheep were at the farm? (*23 + 1 = 24*)

Solution

Choose the Operation

23 + 14 = 37   or   23
                    + 14

                      37

There are 37 purple sheep at the Imaginary Farm.

Related Problems: 58, 54, 42, 34, 22

Problem Extensions

1. Suppose there are only 12 more purple sheep than green sheep. How many purple sheep are at the farm? (*23 + 12 = 35*)

2. Suppose there are 3 fewer purple sheep than green sheep. How many purple sheep are at the Imaginary Farm? (*23 − 3 = 20*)

71 PROCESS PROBLEM

All of the goats at the Imaginary Farm look funny, but Ralph looks the funniest of them all. Ralph always wears an old hat and he wears old shoes on all of his feet. If Ralph could reach his hat, he would eat it. Fortunately, Ralph can't reach his hat. Instead, Ralph eats 3 of his shoes every day! In the morning, the imaginary farmer has to put 3 more shoes on Ralph. If Ralph does this every day, how many shoes does Ralph eat in 1 week?

MATERIALS
counters (at least 21 per group)

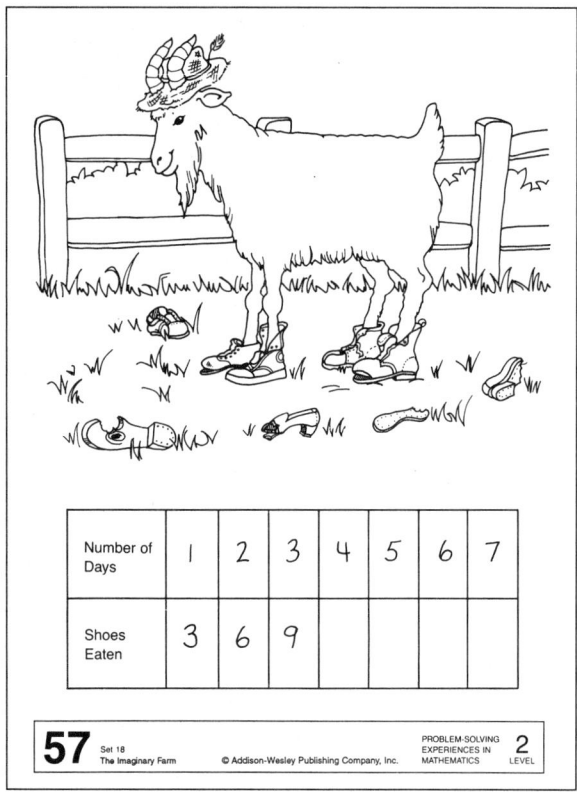

Understanding the Problem

- What kind of animal is Ralph? (*a goat*)
- Why does Ralph look funny? (*he wears an old hat and old shoes*)
- How many old shoes does he wear at a time? (*4*)
- Does Ralph eat his hat? (*no*) Why not? (*he can't reach it*)
- What does Ralph eat? (*his shoes*)
- How many shoes does he eat? (*3 every day*)
- What are we trying to find out about Ralph? (*how many shoes he eats in 1 week*)
- How many days are in 1 week? (*7*)

Solving the Problem

Complete a Table/Look for a Pattern

- What does the top row of numbers in the table tell us? (*the number of days*) The bottom row of numbers? (*the number of shoes eaten after that number of days*)
- After 2 days, what is the total number of shoes Ralph has eaten? (*6*) Can you point to this in the table?
- How many shoes will Ralph have eaten after 4 days? (*12*) How did you find this number? (*add 3 to 9*)
- How do you find the next number to the right on the bottom row of the table? (*add 3 to the previous number*)

Use Manipulatives/Look for a Pattern

- Place your counters into piles of 3 to represent the shoes Ralph eats every day.
- How many piles show the number of shoes Ralph eats in 2 days? (*2*) How many shoes does he eat in 3 days? (*9*) Continue the pattern to find the answer.

STRATEGY ASSESSMENT IDEAS

Listen and watch as students work to see if they

- place numbers correctly in the table
- use a pattern to correctly extend the table
- interpret the table to arrive at the correct answer

Solution

Complete a Table/Look for a Pattern

Number of Days	1	2	3	4	5	6	7
Shoes Eaten	3	6	9	12	15	18	21

Ralph eats 21 shoes in 1 week.

Related Problems: 60, 59, 40, 39, 36

Problem Extensions

1. How many shoes would Ralph have eaten after 10 days? *(30)*
2. Suppose Ralph ate only 2 shoes every day, not 3. How many shoes would Ralph eat in 1 week? *(14)*

72 PROCESS PROBLEM

Chickens at the Imaginary Farm don't act like regular chickens. The chicken named Henny barks like a dog instead of clucking like a regular chicken. Another chicken named Chicky lays flat eggs in funny shapes and in a pattern. The picture you have shows Chicky and the first 4 eggs she laid. Can you see the pattern and draw the next 3 eggs Chicky will lay?

MATERIALS

attribute blocks (or counters or paper shapes) (at least 4 of each shape—circle and square—per group)

Understanding the Problem

- Do the chickens at the Imaginary Farm act like regular chickens? (*no*)
- Does Henny the chicken cluck like a regular chicken? (*no, she barks like a dog*)
- Who lays her eggs in funny shapes? (*Chicky*)
- What shapes are Chicky's eggs? (*circles and squares*)
- Does Chicky lay her eggs in a particular way? (*yes, in a pattern*)

Solving the Problem

Look for a Pattern

- Which shape egg did Chicky lay first? (*circle*) Second? (*square*) Third? (*square*) Fourth? (*circle*)
- Do you see a pattern in the eggs Chicky laid? (*1 circle, 2 squares, 1 circle*)
- If the fifth egg is a square, what will the next be? (*square*)

Use Manipulatives

- Use your shapes to show the pattern that Chicky's eggs have made so far.
- Which shape did Chicky lay first? (*circle*) Second? (*square*) Third? (*square*) Fourth? (*circle*)
- Try using your shapes to see what you think should be next. Tell why.
- If the fifth egg is a square, what will the next egg be? (*square*)
- After using your shapes to continue the pattern correctly, draw the shapes to continue it.

STRATEGY ASSESSMENT IDEAS

Listen and watch as students work to see if they

- describe a pattern formed by the shapes
- extend the pattern correctly
- use the pattern to arrive at the correct answer

Solution

Look for a Pattern

The next 3 eggs will be square, square, circle.

Related Problems: 71, 60, 59, 40, 39

Problem Extension

Find the next 3 shapes to continue the pattern. (draw these shapes on the board)

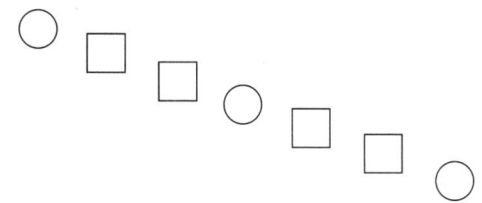

SET 19

Winter Fun

One Sunday afternoon Packy invited several of his friends over to his house to play in the snow. Packy has enough sleds and toboggans that each of his friends could have one to ride on.

Just behind Packy's house is a long, steep hill that's great for riding down on a sled or a toboggan. Some of Packy's friends had never been on a sled or a toboggan before and didn't know what to do. Packy helped each of them learn to ride a sled and a toboggan. He even rode down the hill with them several times so they would not be afraid. Packy remembers that he was afraid the first time he rode down the hill, and he didn't want his friends to get scared.

Packy and his friends played on the hill for several hours. When it was time to go home, they were all very tired and very, very cold, but everyone had fun and wanted to play on the hill again next week.

Discussion Questions

1. What did Packy invite several of his friends to his house to do? (*play in the snow*)
2. What is the difference between a sled and a toboggan? (*see Blackline Master 59*)
3. Why did Packy ride down the hill with his friends? (*yes*)
4. How did the children feel when it was time to go home? (*tired and cold, but they wanted to come again*)
5. Have you ever gone sledding? What did you do?

73 SKILL ACTIVITY

Tell a Question

Possible Addition Questions

1. How much does it cost to rent skates for 1 hour and a sled for 1 hour?
2. How much does it cost to rent a sled and a toboggan for 1 hour each?
3. How much does it cost to rent a rubber tire for 2 hours?

Possible Subtraction Questions

1. How much more does it cost to rent skates for 1 hour than to rent a toboggan for 1 hour?
2. If you rented a sled for 1 hour and gave the cashier 50¢, how much money should you get back?
3. If you have 20¢, how much more money do you need to rent a toboggan for 1 hour?

TEACHING ACTIONS

1. Discuss Blackline Master 60 with the students. Be sure they understand all of the words on the sign.
2. Have students tell any questions they can answer using data from the picture. Solicit a variety of questions.
3. (*optional*) Have students answer some of the questions.

74 ONE-STEP PROBLEM

All of the children sledding went into Packy's house two times during the afternoon to warm up. The first time they were inside, Packy's father served 6 cups of hot apple cider. The second time they came inside they all said they were "freezing," so Packy's father served 13 cups of hot apple cider! How many cups of hot apple cider did Packy's father serve altogether during the afternoon?

Understanding the Problem

- How many times did the children go into Packy's house? (*2 times*)
- Why did they go inside? (*to warm up from sledding*)
- What did Packy's father serve to the children? (*hot apple cider*)
- How many cups of hot apple cider did Packy's father serve the first time the children went inside? (*6*) The second time? (*13*)
- Why did he serve more cups the second time? (*they were "freezing"*)
- What are we trying to find? (*how many cups of hot apple cider were served altogether*)

Solving the Problem

- If 2 cups were served the first time and 3 the second time, how many were served altogether? (*5*) How did you find this answer? (*add*)
- If you want to find the total number of cups, which operation should you use? (*addition*)

Solution

Choose the Operation

6 + 13 = 19   or   6
                     + 13

                      19

Packy's father served 19 cups of hot apple cider.

Related Problems: 70, 58, 54, 42, 34

Problem Extension

How many more cups did Packy's father serve the second time than the first time? (*13 − 6 = 7*)

75 PROCESS PROBLEM

Carl, Jana, Sue Ellen, and Packy all went down the hill on their sleds. They went down in a line one right behind the other. Sue Ellen went down first, and Jana went last. Packy went down behind Carl. Who went down second?en went down first, and Jana went last. Packy went down behind Carl. Who went down second?

MATERIALS

cubes or counters (4 different colors per group)

Understanding the Problem

- What did Carl, Jana, Sue Ellen, and Packy do? (*went down the hill on their sleds*)
- How did they go down the hill? (*in a line*)
- Who went down first? (*Sue Ellen*)
- What do we know about Jana? (*she went down last*)
- What are we trying to find out about these sledders? (*who went down second*)

Solving the Problem

Logical Reasoning

- Who went down first? (*Sue Ellen*) Write Sue Ellen's name beside the first child.
- Who went down last? (*Jana*) Write Jana's name beside the last child.
- Use the other information to decide which names to write beside the 2 remaining children.

Use Manipulatives

- Use the cubes to show what this information tells you. Choose what color you would like each child's jacket to be. Put a matching cube on each child.
- Who went down first? (*Sue Ellen*) Put the cube for the first child next to Sue Ellen in the list of names.
- What other information do you know? Move each cube to show what this information tells you.

Solution

Use Logical Reasoning

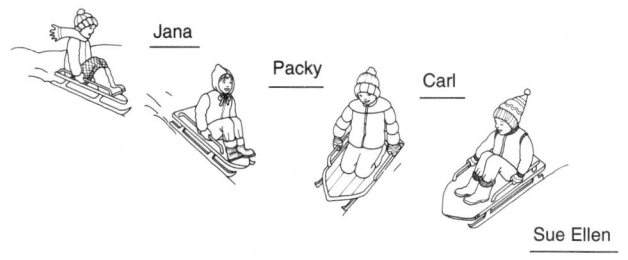

Related Problems: 64, 63, 56, 52, 51

Problem Extension

Suppose Packy went down ahead of Carl. Who came in second? (*Packy*)

STRATEGY ASSESSMENT IDEAS

Listen and watch as students work to see if they

- use a plan to place the counters and to record their work
- correctly use all conditions given in the problem
- arrive at correct conclusions through reasoning

76 ▷ PROCESS PROBLEM

A group of children took 5 toboggans down a steep hill. One child was on the first toboggan, 3 children were on the second toboggan, and 5 children were on the third toboggan. How many children do you think rode the fourth toboggan? The fifth toboggan?

MATERIALS
cubes or counters (25–30 per pair)

Understanding the Problem

- What did the children do on the steep hill? (*rode down on toboggans*)
- What is a toboggan?
- Did the same number of children go down the hill on each toboggan? (*no*)
- How many went down on the first toboggan? (*1*) The second? (*3*) The third? (*5*)
- What are we trying to find? (*how many children went down the hill on the fourth and fifth toboggans*)

Solving the Problem

Look for a Pattern

- How many more children went down on the second toboggan than on the first toboggan? (*2 more*)
- How many more went down on the third toboggan than on the second toboggan? (*2 more*)
- Do you see a pattern in the number of children on each toboggan? (*2 more than the one ahead of it*)

Use Manipulatives

- Place a cube on each child in the picture.
- Arrange the cubes to create a chart (see below). Use the cube from the first sled in row one, cubes from the second sled in a second row, and so on.

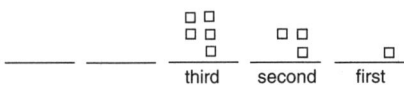

- Use the chart to answer the following:

  How many more children went down on the second toboggan then on the first toboggan? (*2 more*)

  How many more went down on the third toboggan than on the second toboggan? (*2 more*)

  Do you see a pattern in the number of children on each toboggan? (*2 more than the one ahead of it*)

  ▶ *turn the page*

STRATEGY ASSESSMENT IDEAS

Listen and watch as students work to see if they

- describe a pattern formed by the picture
- extend the pattern correctly
- use the pattern to arrive at the correct answer
- place cubes correctly in the table (if table is made)

Solution

Look for a Pattern

7 children rode the fourth toboggan, and
9 children rode the fifth toboggan.

Related Problems: 72, 71, 60, 59, 40

Problem Extensions

1. What was the total number of children who rode down the hill on all 5 of the toboggans? (*25*)

2. Suppose 2 children went down on the first toboggan, 4 on the second, and 6 on the third. How many rode on the fourth and fifth toboggans? (*8 on the fourth and 10 on the fifth*)

Davy Crockett

Davy Crockett was an American pioneer, an army scout, a politician, and a hunter. He was good at all of these things, and that made him a famous symbol of the American frontier. Davy Crockett was born in the state of Tennessee in 1786. He had 5 brothers and 3 sisters.

There are many stories about Davy Crockett. Some are true, but some are make-believe. One of the make-believe stories about him is that he rode up a waterfall (Niagara Falls) standing on an alligator's back! Other stories about Davy Crockett say that he could jump higher, run faster, and hold his breath longer than any one else in the whole country.

Davy Crockett was elected to Congress (in Washington, D.C.) to represent the people in Tennessee. After he left Congress, Davy Crockett went to Texas. People from Texas were fighting people from Mexico over who should own the land. Davy Crockett died during a big battle at a fort called the Alamo.

Discussion Questions

1. Was Davy Crockett a real person? (*yes*)
2. Why was Davy Crockett famous? (*he was a good pioneer, army scout, politician, and hunter*)
3. Are all the stories about Davy Crockett true? (*no*)
4. What was Davy Crockett elected to? (*Congress*)
5. Where did Davy Crockett die? (*in Texas at a fort called the Alamo*)

77 SKILL ACTIVITY

Tell a Story Problem

Setting
Every morning Davy Crockett goes for a walk in the woods.

Number Sentence A
9 + 6 = ?

Possible Story Problem for Number Sentence A
One morning when Davy Crockett was walking through the woods, he saw 9 deer standing in a field and 6 deer running through the woods. How many deer did Davy Crockett see on his walk through the woods that morning?

Number Sentence B
4 + 2 = ?

Possible Story Problem for Number Sentence B
One morning when Davy Crockett was walking through the woods, he saw the footprints of a deer and the footprints of a turkey. How many footprints did he see in all? (*Note:* A deer has 4 legs and a turkey has 2 legs.)

TEACHING ACTIONS

1. Read the story setting.
2. Have students tell a story problem that would be solved using Number Sentence A.
3. Repeat for Number Sentence B.
4. (*optional*) Have students solve their story problems.

78 ONE-STEP PROBLEM

One day Davy Crockett was walking in the woods when he heard a noise. He stopped walking, and looked around. There were 22 deer in front of him and 34 deer behind him. Davy Crockett knew he was not in danger, so he watched the deer for a while and then went on walking. How many deer did Davy Crockett see in the woods altogether?

Understanding the Problem

- What made Davy Crockett stop when he was walking in the woods? (*he heard a noise*)
- What did he see? (*deer*)
- Where were the deer? (*in front of him and behind him*)
- How many deer were in front of him? (*22*) Behind him? (*34*)
- What did Davy Crockett do when he saw the deer? (*watched them, then continued walking*)
- What are we trying to find? (*how many deer Davy Crockett saw in all*)

Solving the Problem

- If Davy Crockett saw 2 deer in front of him and 3 deer behind him, how many deer did he see altogether? (*5*) Which operation did you use to find that answer? (*addition*)
- Since you want to find the total number of deer, should you add or subtract? (*add*)

Solution

Choose the Operation

22 + 34 = 56   or   22
                      + 34

                        56

Davy Crockett saw a total of 56 deer.

Related Problems: 74, 70, 58, 54, 42

Problem Extension

How many more deer were behind Davy Crockett than were in front of him? (*34 − 22 = 12*)

79 PROCESS PROBLEM

One day when Davy Crockett was on his way home, he stopped at the trading post to buy 1 sack of vegetables and 1 bag of fruit. There are 6 different ways Davy Crockett can buy 1 of the vegetables and 1 of the fruits. Can you list the 6 ways?

MATERIALS

attribute blocks (1 set per 12 students) or 12 pattern blocks (2 of each kind per student)

Understanding the Problem

- Where did Davy Crockett stop on his way home? (*at the trading post*)
- Did he want to buy 2 sacks of vegetables? (*no*) 2 bags of fruit? (*no*)
- What did he want to buy? (*1 sack of vegetables and 1 bag of fruit*)
- What vegetables did he have to choose from? (*corn, beans, peas*)
- What fruits did he have to choose from? (*pears, plums*)
- How many different ways can he buy 1 vegetable and 1 fruit? (*6*)

Solving the Problem

Complete an Organized List

- If Davy Crockett picked corn, name 1 fruit he could choose. (*pears or plums*) Can you name another fruit he could have chosen?
- Pick 1 vegetable. Now pick 1 fruit. Write these on the tags at the bottom of the page. Now can you pick another vegetable and fruit?

Use Manipulatives

- Have students place a different pattern block on each fruit and vegetable for reference.
- Suppose Davy Crockett picked corn. Place a pattern block representing corn in one of the squares. Name one fruit he could choose. (*pears or plums*) Put the pattern block for that fruit in the circle next to the square for corn.
  - What other fruit could he use with corn? (*plum or pear, whichever wasn't named first*)
  - Can you use your pattern blocks to find all the different ways he can buy 1 vegetable and 1 fruit?

STRATEGY ASSESSMENT IDEAS

Listen and watch as students work to see if they

- create correct entries for their lists
- organize entries in their lists
- list all possibilities

Solution

Complete an Organized List

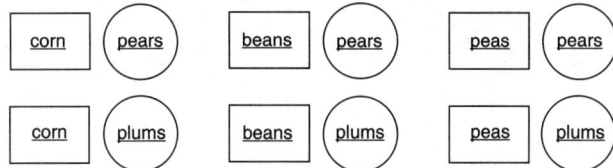

Related Problems: 67, 55, 28, 27, 7

Problem Extensions

1. Suppose there was a fourth vegetable, carrots. Now how many different ways could Davy Crockett have picked 1 vegetable and 1 fruit? (*8*)

2. Suppose there were 3 vegetables and 3 fruits. Now how many different ways could he have picked 1 vegetable and 1 fruit? (*9*)

80 PROCESS PROBLEM

Davy Crockett went into town on a Saturday morning to buy some supplies that he had needed for a long time. He had saved his money, and now he had enough to buy what he needed. He bought 3 items at the store and spent $13. Which 3 items did Davy Crockett buy?

Understanding the Problem

- Why did Davy Crockett go into town Saturday? (*to buy supplies*)
- What are supplies?
- How many items did he buy at the store? (*3*)
- How much did he spend altogether? (*$13*)
- How much did a box of candles cost? (*$4*)
- What cost $2? (*a belt*)
- What are we trying to find? (*which 3 items Davy Crockett bought*)

Solving the Problem

- Could Davy Crockett have bought a hat, candles, and a belt? (*no, he only spent $13*)
- Could he have bought only moccasins and a shirt? (*no, he bought 3 items*)
- Can you guess which 3 items he bought and then check your guess by adding?

Solution

Guess and Check

- Try hat, candles, belt: 8 + 4 + 2 = $14 (*too high*)
- Try candles, belt, shirt: 4 + 2 + 6 = $12 (*too low*)
- Try candles, moccasins, belt: 4 + 7 + 2 = $13 (*correct*)
- Try candles, shirt, salt: 4 + 6 + 3 = $13 (*correct*)
- Try hat, belt, salt: 8 + 2 + 3 = $14 (*correct*)

Davy Crockett could have bought any one of these combinations of 3 items: (1) candles, moccasins, belt; (2) candles, shirt, salt; or (3) hat, belt, salt.

Note: Encourage students to find all 3 possible combinations.

Related Problems: 56, 32, 31, 8, 7

Problem Extension

Suppose Davy Crockett bought 3 items and paid $15. What did he buy? (*moccasins, belt, shirt; or hat, candles, salt*)

STRATEGY ASSESSMENT IDEAS

Listen and watch as students work to see if they

- make a reasonable first guess (students should choose 3 different items)
- make a second guess using what they learn from checking the first guess

SET 21

Eduardo's Collection

It was Tuesday, the day Eduardo had been waiting for. Tuesday was sharing day in his classroom. There was a problem, however. Eduardo could not decide what he wanted to share with his classmates.

"Why don't you take your new black race car?" asked Eduardo's mother.

"I really don't want the other kids to play with it," Eduardo said. "Someone might break it."

His mother said, "Well then, how about your teddy bear?"

"No way, mom!" said Eduardo. "The kids might think I'm a baby."

Eduardo thought and thought, but he just couldn't think of anything to take to school to share with his classmates. At the last minute, as he was just about to leave his house for school on Tuesday morning, Eduardo grabbed his race car and rushed out the door. "I just won't let anyone touch it," he thought to himself.

When it was Eduardo's turn to share, he carefully carried his race car to the front of the class. "This is my new black race car," he said.

"Oh, wow! Can we see it?" "Can we play with it?" "Let me see it!" All the children were anxious to play with Eduardo's beautiful race car.

"Well," Eduardo hesitated. "I guess you can see it. But be careful." When he saw how happy it made the other children, he decided that maybe it was OK to share his new toy after all. And it turned out that everyone was very careful. Eduardo's fancy black race car came back to him in perfect shape.

Discussion Questions

1. What day was sharing day in Eduardo's classroom? (*Tuesday*)
2. What did Eduardo's mother suggest that Eduardo take? (*black race car, teddy bear*)

3. Why didn't Eduardo want to take his race car? (*the other kids might break it*)
4. Why didn't Eduardo want to take his teddy bear? (*the other kids might think he was a baby*)
5. What did Eduardo finally take to school? (*black race car*)
6. What did his classmates think about his car? (*they liked it*)
7. Would you share a new toy with your classmates?
8. How would you feel if someone broke one of your new toys?

81 SKILL ACTIVITY

Complete a Picture to Show a Story

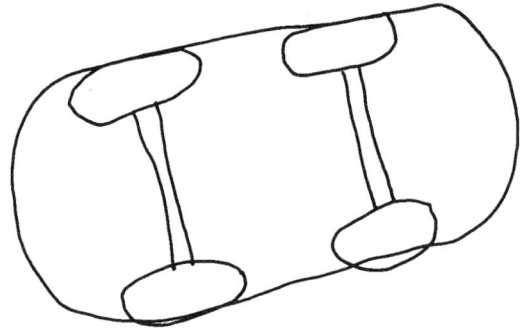

Story

Eduardo collects toy cars—race cars, family cars, jeeps, and trucks. Each car has 4 wheels. Eduardo has 5 cars in all.

TEACHING ACTIONS

1. Draw a picture of a car on the board (be sure all 4 wheels can be seen). Have the children copy it. Tell them, "This is one of Eduardo's toy cars; see the 4 wheels."
2. Read the story to the students and have them draw the other cars. (Be sure they show 4 wheels on each car.)
3. Show different students' pictures.
4. (optional) Ask students to find how many wheels there are on 5 cars.

82 ONE-STEP PROBLEM

There are 28 children in Eduardo's second-grade classroom. On sharing day Eduardo thought that some children were absent. He counted all the children in the classroom. There were 21 children in all. How many children were absent on sharing day?

Understanding the Problem

- What grade is Eduardo in? (*second*)
- How many children are in Eduardo's class? (*28*)
- What did Eduardo do when he thought some children were absent? (*he counted all the children*)
- What does it mean to be absent? (*you are not in class on that day*)
- How many children did he count? (*21*)
- Do you think Eduardo counted himself? (*yes*)
- Are we trying to find how many children are in Eduardo's class? (*no*)
- Are we trying to find how many children were in class on sharing day? (*no, how many were absent*)

Solving the Problem

- If there were only 4 children in Eduardo's class and Eduardo counted 2, how many children were absent? (*2*)
- Were some of the children missing on sharing day? (*yes*) How can we find how many? (*subtract or count on*)
- Do you use addition or subtraction to solve this problem? (*subtraction*)
- Can you write a number sentence for this problem? (*see solution*)

Solution

Choose the Operation

$$28 - 21 = 7 \quad \text{or} \quad \begin{array}{r} 28 \\ -21 \\ \hline 7 \end{array}$$

7 children were absent on sharing day.

Related Problems: 66, 62, 50, 46, 38

Problem Extension

Twenty-four children were in class on sharing day and 21 brought things from home to share with the class. How many children did not bring something to share with the class? (*take-away subtraction: 24 − 21 = 3 children did not bring anything*)

83 TWO-STEP PROBLEM

Eduardo collects toy cars. He also collects pictures of famous antique cars and fast racing cars. Eduardo has 5 pictures of antique cars and 3 pictures of racing cars. How many pictures has Eduardo collected?

Eduardo paid 2¢ for each car picture in his collection. How much did he pay for the pictures he has?

Understanding the Problem

- What does Eduardo collect besides toy cars? (*pictures of cars*)
- What is an antique car? (*a very old car; an old-fashioned car*)
- How many pictures of antique cars does Eduardo have? (*5*)
- How many pictures of racing cars does he have? (*3*)
- How much did Eduardo pay for each picture? (*2¢*)

Solving the Problem

- How many pictures of cars does Eduardo have? (*5 + 3 = 8*)
- To find how many pictures of cars Eduardo has do you put together his antique card pictures and racing car pictures? (*yes*) What operation do you use when you put together? (*addition*)
- Did he pay the same amount for each car picture? (*yes*) How much? (*2¢*)
- If Eduardo paid 2¢ for 1 picture, how much did he pay for 2 pictures? (*4¢*) 3 pictures? (*6¢*) Can you count by 2s and write down what you say?
- Which operation can you use to find the total amount he paid? (*either addition or multiplication*)

Solution

Choose the Operation

- Addition and Addition

    5 + 3 = 8 pictures of cars

    2¢ + 2¢ + 2¢ + 2¢ + 2¢ + 2¢ + 2¢ + 2¢ = 16¢

- Addition and Multiplication

    5 + 3 = 8 pictures of cars

    8 × 2¢ = 16¢

He paid 16¢ for 8 pictures.

Problem Extension

Suppose Eduardo had 5 pictures of antique cars and 4 pictures of racing cars. How many pictures does he have? (*9*) If the pictures cost 3¢ each, how much did Eduardo pay for all his pictures? (*5 + 4 = 9; 9 × 3¢ = 27¢*)

84 PROCESS PROBLEM

Eduardo likes to line up his toy cars on the table in his bedroom. Eduardo has 5 cars in all. His antique car is between his jeep and his blue race car. His fire truck is between his antique car and his blue race car. His blue race car is between his fire truck and his yellow race car. How does Eduardo have his cars lined up on the table?

MATERIALS

black, green, yellow, red, and blue cubes (1 of each color per group)

Understanding the Problem

- What does Eduardo like to do with his toy cars? (*line them up on a table*)
- How many cars does he have? (*5*)
- Point to the Eduardo's antique car.
- Is his antique car between his jeep and his blue race car? (*yes*)
- What 2 cars is his fire truck between? (*antique car and blue race car*)
- What car is between his fire truck and his yellow race car? (*blue race car*)
- What do we want to find out about the toy cars? (*how Eduardo has lined them up*)

Solving the Problem

Use Manipulatives

- How are the 2 race cars different? (*one is blue and the other is yellow*) Use a blue cube to represent one race car and a yellow cube to represent the other. Choose 3 other color cubes to represent the fire truck, the antique car, and the jeep.
- The first clue is: "His antique car is between his jeep and his blue race car." Use your cubes to show this.
- Listen to the other clues again, and place your cubes in the correct place to show where the cars would be.

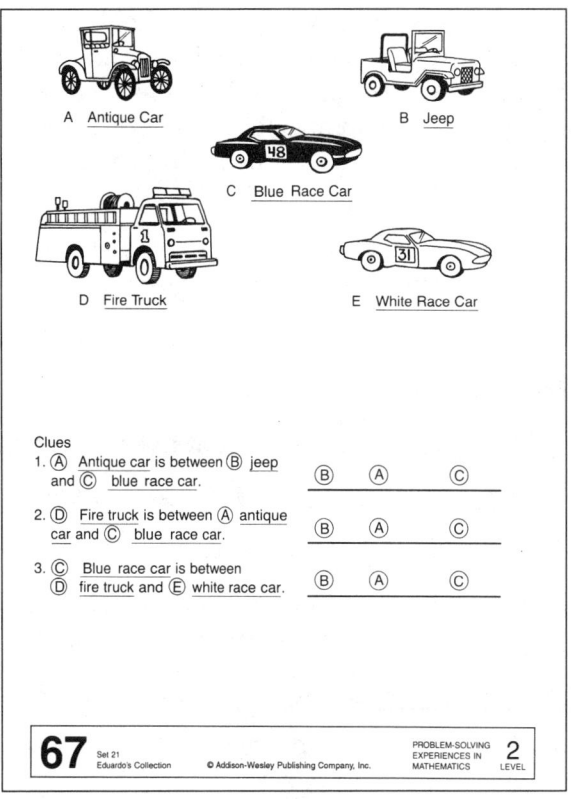

Solution

Use Logical Reasoning

(B)(A)(C)   A is between B and C
(B)(A)(D)(C)   D is between A and C
(B)(A)(D)(C)(E)   C is between D and E

Related Problems: 75, 64, 63, 56, 52

Problem Extension

Eduardo collects pictures of cars. He has more pictures of racing cars than fire trucks. He has fewer pictures of jeeps than fire trucks. Which cars does he have more pictures of, racing cars or jeeps? (*racing cars*)

STRATEGY ASSESSMENT IDEAS

Listen and watch as students work to see if they

- use a plan to arrange the cubes and to record their work
- correctly use all conditions given in the problem
- arrive at correct conclusions through reasoning

85 > PROCESS PROBLEM

Eduardo's teacher, Mr. Williams, told the class they were going to play a game. "I will put on my desk the things 5 of us brought to share. Each student will give the class a clue about what he or she brought. The rest of you must find out which thing each of the 5 students brought."

Note: Refer students to Blackline Master 68. Read clues slowly as students look at the picture.

Clues:

Melissa said, "You can wear what I brought."

Rodney said, "What I brought lives in a cage."

Carrie's clue was, "I can bounce what I brought."

Carlos said, "What I brought is good to eat."

Julie said, "I can't think of a good clue. Maybe everyone can still figure out what I brought."

Understanding the Problem

- What did Eduardo's teacher tell the class they were going to do? (*play a game*)
- What did he put on his desk? (*5 things brought by the students for sharing day*)
- What is a clue? (*a little information to help you find out about something*)
- Did each of the 5 children give a clue? (*no, only 4 of them did*)
- Who did not give a clue? (*Julie*)

Solving the Problem

- Read the names of the children to students.
- Can you draw a line from Melissa's name to the thing she brought?
- Can you draw a line from Rodney's name to the thing he brought? Can you do the same for Carrie and Carlos?
- How many things are left? (*1*) Who must have brought it? (*Julie*)

STRATEGY ASSESSMENT IDEAS

Listen and watch as students work to see if they

- use the picture appropriately to solve the problem
- correctly use all conditions given in the problem
- arrive at correct conclusions through reasoning

Solution

Use Logical Reasoning/Use a Picture

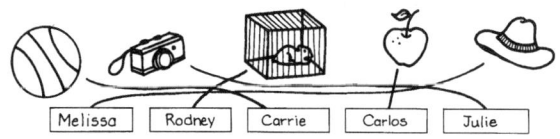

Related Problems: 84, 75, 64, 63, 56

Problem Extension

Eduardo asked Rodney how old his gerbil was. Rodney said, "He is less than 20 weeks old and more than 15 weeks old. When you count by 2s you can get his age. His age is closer to 15 than 20." How old is Rodney's gerbil? (*16 weeks old*)

SET 22

Picnic in the Park

One warm Saturday afternoon, the twins, Annie and Chris, were very bored. They could not think of anything interesting to do. They went to their parents for ideas. "What can we do that's fun?" asked Annie. "Yeah," said Chris, "we're bored. What can we do?"

"Well," said Mom, "why don't we pack a picnic lunch and take a hike in the woods?"

"Great idea," Dad added. "I need some exercise, and a walk in the woods would be good for all of us."

Chris and his mom began preparing the food. They made 2 kinds of sandwiches—tuna fish and cheese. They also made some potato salad and packed apples and grapes. Chris made some lemonade because he knew everyone would be thirsty after a long hike.

Annie and her dad got the picnic basket from the garage and found an old tablecloth that could be spread out on the ground when they were ready to eat the picnic lunch.

At last they were ready to go. They piled into the car and drove to the state park about 15 miles away. When they got to the park, they started hiking along one of the trails. While they were walking Chris saw 2 raccoons, Annie saw a deer and a woodpecker, and Mom saw an owl. Dad thought the yellow and purple wildflowers were beautiful. Mom smelled some wild ginger. After they had hiked for about 45 minutes, they decided to stop and have their picnic.

The twins spotted a nice, open grassy area under a big, old maple tree. While they were enjoying their lunch, Annie said, "Dad, what are those pretty green plants over there with 3 leaves?"

"You didn't touch them, did you?" asked Dad. When Annie shook her head, Dad said, "Good, because that's poison ivy!"

Discussion Questions

1. What did Chris and Annie's mom suggest they all do? (*pack a picnic and take a hike*)
2. Chris and Annie are twins. What are twins?
3. Where did they decide to go for the picnic? (*state park*)
4. How far away was the state park from their home? (*15 miles*)
5. What did Chris see on the hike? (*2 raccoons*) What did Annie see? (*deer and woodpecker*)
6. What did the twins' mom smell? (*wild ginger*)
7. Did Chris and Annie pick a good spot?
8. What is poison ivy?
9. Have you ever gone on a hike or a picnic?

86 SKILL ACTIVITY

Tell the Operation for a Story Problem

Problem A

Chris and his mom made sandwiches for the picnic to the state park. They made tuna fish sandwiches and cheese sandwiches. They also made some lemonade and packed apples and grapes in the picnic basket. How many sandwiches did they make?

Numbers: 5 tuna fish sandwiches, 7 cheese sandwiches

Problem B

The state park is 15 miles from the family's home. After they had driven part of the distance, Annie asked, "How much farther is the park?" Help Annie figure it out. How many more miles do they have to drive to get to the state park?

Number: 6 miles

Notes

1. Focus on choosing the correct operation to solve a problem, not on solving it.
2. The type of subtraction in Problem B is called missing addend subtraction (for example, 6 + ? = 15 or 15 − 6 = ?). (Refer to Skill Activity 61.)

TEACHING ACTIONS

1. Read and discuss Problem A.
2. Ask students: "If we know how many tuna fish sandwiches and how many cheese sandwiches were made, what would we do to find the total number of sandwiches?" (Give students numbers.)
3. Point out that when the problem involves joining or putting together groups, we use addition to find the total.
4. Read and discuss Problem B.
5. Ask students: "If we know how far they had driven, how could we decide how much farther the state park was?" (Give students the numbers.)
6. Point out that when we want to find how much more or how much farther, we subtract.
7. (optional) Have students solve the 2 problems.

87 ONE-STEP PROBLEM

Chris thought the best thing in the picnic basket was the grapes. Chris loves grapes. Chris ate more grapes than anyone else. Annie said, "Chris, leave some for me! You have had 27 grapes. I've only had 5 grapes." How many more grapes did Chris eat than Annie?

Understanding the Problem

- What did Chris think was the best thing in the picnic basket? (*grapes*)
- Who ate the most grapes? (*Chris*)
- How many grapes did he eat? (*27*)
- How many grapes did Annie eat? (*5*)

Solving the Problem

- Are you asked to find how many grapes Chris and Annie ate all together? (*no*) What are you asked to find? (*how many more grapes Chris ate than Annie*)
- If Chris ate 7 grapes and Annie ate 5 grapes, how many more did Chris eat than Annie? (*2*)
- Is this an addition problem or a subtraction problem? (*subtraction*)
- Can you write a subtraction sentence for this problem? (*see solution*)

Solution

Choose the Operation

$$27 - 5 = 22 \quad \text{or} \quad \begin{array}{r} 27 \\ - 5 \\ \hline 22 \end{array}$$

Chris ate 22 more grapes than Annie ate.

Related Problems: 82, 66, 62, 50, 46

Problem Extension

During the walk, the family saw 16 animals. Annie saw 5 animals. How many animals did the rest of the family see? (*16 − 5 = 11; the rest of the family saw 11 animals*)

88 TWO-STEP PROBLEM

Chris and his mom packed 3 red apples and 2 green apples in the picnic basket. They also packed 12 sandwiches, lemonade, 4 oranges, and a bunch of grapes. How many apples did they pack in the picnic basket?

Chris' mom bought the red and green apples they took on the picnic at the vegetable stand. She paid 3¢ for each apple. How much did she pay for the apples altogether?

Understanding the Problem
- How many red apples were packed in the picnic basket? (*3*)
- How many green apples were packed? (*2*)
- What else was packed? (*12 sandwiches, lemonade, 4 oranges, and grapes*)
- Where did Chris's mom get the apples? (*at the vegetable stand*)
- How much did she pay for each apple? (*3¢*)

Solving the Problem
- How many apples in total were packed in the picnic basket? (*5*)
- The red and green apples were put together in the picnic basket. What operation do you use when you put together? (*addition*)
- Did each apple cost the same amount? (*yes*) How much? (*3¢*)
- If 1 apple cost 3¢, how much did 2 apples cost? (*6¢*) 3 apples? (*9¢*) Can you count by 3s and write down what you say?
- Which operation can you use to find the total cost of the apples? (*either addition or multiplication*)

Solution
Choose the Operations
- Addition and Addition
  3 + 2 = 5 number of apples packed
  3¢ + 3¢ + 3¢ + 3¢ + 3¢ = 15¢
- Addition and Multiplication
  3 + 2 = 5
  5 × 3¢ = 15¢

The apples cost a total of 15¢.

Related Problem: 83

Problem Extension

Suppose 4 red apples and 3 green apples were packed, and each apple cost 4¢ at the grocery store. How much did all the apples cost? (*4 + 3 = 7; 7 × 4¢ = 28¢*)

89 > PROCESS PROBLEM

The picnic lunch that Chris, Annie, and their parents took with them had sandwiches and fruit. There were 2 kinds of sandwiches—tuna and cheese. There were 3 kinds of fruit—apples, oranges, and grapes. Annie decided to have 1 kind of fruit and 1 kind of sandwich. There are 6 different ways Annie can choose 1 fruit and 1 sandwich. Can you list the 6 ways?

MATERIALS

pattern blocks in 5 shapes (2 of each per group)

Understanding the Problem

- How many kinds of sandwiches were there? (*2—tuna and cheese*) How many kinds of fruit were there? (*3—apples, oranges, and grapes*)
- What did Annie decide to have? (*1 kind of sandwich and 1 kind of fruit*)
- How many ways did Annie have to choose from? (*6 ways*)

Solving the Problem

Complete an Organized List

- Look at the picture. If Annie picked grapes, can you name 1 sandwich she could choose? (*cheese or tuna*)
- What is another sandwich she could choose? Pick 1 fruit. Now pick 1 sandwich. Write these in the first 2 spaces.
- Now can you pick another pair? Can you list all 6 ways?

Use Manipulatives

- Use a different shape for each sandwich and fruit.
- Put a shape on each picture. Move the other shapes around and make pairs to show the ways to put sandwiches and fruit together.
- Can you find 6 different ways? (*Remember that a fruit and sandwich must go together, not 2 fruits or 2 sandwiches.*)

▶ *turn the page*

STRATEGY ASSESSMENT IDEAS

Listen and watch as students work to see if they

- create correct entries for their lists
- organize entries in their lists
- list all possibilities

Solution

Complete an Organized List

| grapes | and | cheese | | apples | and | cheese |
| grapes | and | tuna | | apples | and | tuna |

| | oranges | and | cheese |
| | oranges | and | tuna |

Related Problems: 79, 67, 55, 28, 27

Problem Extensions

1. Suppose that in addition to grapes, apples, and oranges, there was a fourth kind of fruit—pears. Now how many different ways could Annie pick 1 fruit and 1 sandwich? *(8)*

2. Suppose there were 3 fruits and a third kind of sandwich—peanut butter. Now how many different ways could Annie pick 1 fruit and 1 sandwich? *(9)*

90 PROCESS PROBLEM

On the ride home from their picnic at the state park, Annie said, "Let's play a game."

"I've got a game for you," Dad said. "I'm thinking of three different numbers. When you add them together you get 17. The numbers are bigger than 2 and less than 9. What three numbers am I thinking of?"

Use the numbers shown in your picture to find what three numbers he was thinking of.

Understanding the Problem

- What did Annie suggest they do on the ride home? (*play a game*)
- How many numbers did Dad think of? (*3*)
- Were the numbers all different? (*yes*)
- How much did the three numbers add up to? (*17*)
- Could 2 be one of the numbers? (*no, they were bigger than 2*)
- Could one of the numbers be 9? (*no, the numbers were less than 9*)
- Could 3 + 7 + 8 be the answer? (*no, the sum is too high*)

Solving the Problem

- Try any three numbers. What do they add up to?
- If 3 is one of the numbers, what could the other two numbers be? (*see solution*)
- Could 3 and 4 be two of the numbers? (*no*)
- If 8 is one of the numbers, what could the other two numbers be? (*3 and 6 or 4 and 5*)

Solution

Guess and Check/Use Logical Reasoning

Try 3 numbers:

- 3 + 4 + 5 = 12 (*too low*)
- 3 + 4 + 8 = 15 (*still too low, need 2 more*)
- 3 + 6 + 8 = 17 (*correct*)

The numbers were 3, 6, and 8.

Note: 4, 5, 8 and 4, 6, 7 also add up to 17. The emphasis in this problem should be on using reasoning to make good guesses.

Related Problems: 85, 84, 80, 75, 68

Problem Extension

The family played another game. This time Chris thought of three different numbers. "My three numbers add up to 12 and they are between 2 and 9." What three numbers was Chris thinking of? (*3, 4, and 5*)

STRATEGY ASSESSMENT IDEAS

Listen and watch as students work to see if they

- make a reasonable first guess (students should choose three numbers, all bigger than 2 and less than 9)
- make a second guess using what they learn from checking their first guess
- check their answer to be sure all the information was used

Mailing a Letter

On Saturday mornings, Wanda goes with her father to the post office to mail letters and sometimes a package. After her father pays the postal worker for the postage on a package, the postal worker places the package in a big cart with a lot of other packages. Then Wanda and her father leave. Wanda has always wondered what happens to the packages after she leaves. Next week Wanda will find out what happens to the packages, because Wanda's class is going on a trip to visit the post office!

Wanda's teacher, Mr. Mason, told the students they could each bring a letter that they wanted to send to a special friend. Of course it had to be in an envelope with a stamp and the address on it. Mr. Mason told them that a postal worker was going to show them exactly what happens to letters and packages when they are mailed at the post office.

Wanda wrote a long letter to her grandfather, telling him about what she would see at the post office next week. When Wanda goes to the post office with her class, she will mail her letter to her special friend, her grandfather.

Discussion Questions

1. Where does Wanda go with her father on Saturday mornings? (*post office*)
2. After Wanda and her father leave the post office, what does Wanda wonder about? (*what happens to the packages*)
3. How will Wanda find out what happens to letters and packages at the post office? (*she will take a class trip to the post office*)
4. Who is the special friend that Wanda will mail a letter to? (*her grandfather*)
5. If you were going to mail a letter to a special friend, who would it be?

91 SKILL ACTIVITY

Tell Missing Data

Problem A
Boys and girls rode in a bus on the class visit to the post office. Seven boys rode in the bus. What was the total number of children who rode in the bus?

Problem B
Each mail truck has its own parking place at the post office. When Wanda arrived at the post office, only 4 mail trucks were parked. How many mail truck parking places are at the post office Wanda visited?

TEACHING ACTIONS

1. Read Problem A to the students. Ask, "Can you solve this problem?"
2. Discuss what information they need to know to solve this problem.
3. (*optional*) Have students make up reasonable data for the problem.
4. (*optional*) Have students solve the problem.
5. Repeat for Problem B.

92 ONE-STEP PROBLEM

Wanda wanted to mail two pictures she had painted. One picture was for her grandfather, and the other was for her friend, Lisa, whom she'd met last summer on their vacation. She needed envelopes for the picture. She wasn't sure what size of envelope each picture would need, so she asked the postal worker. The postal worker said one of the pictures could be mailed in an envelope that cost 20¢, but the other was bigger and needed a 37¢ envelope. Wanda bought an envelope for each picture. How much did she have to pay for both envelopes?

Understanding the Problem
- What did Wanda want to do at the post office? (*mail 2 pictures she had painted*)
- To whom was she mailing the pictures? (*her grandfather and a friend, Lisa*)
- What wasn't Wanda sure about? (*what size envelope each picture would need*)
- How much was each envelope she bought? (*20¢ and 37¢*)

Solving the Problem
- Are you comparing the cost of the 2 envelopes, or are you trying to find the total? (*trying to find the total*)
- If you want to find the total amount of money Wanda spent, should you add or subtract? (*add*)

Solution
Choose the Operation

20¢ + 37¢ = 57¢   or   20¢
                         + 37¢

                           57¢

Wanda paid 57¢ for the 2 envelopes.

Related Problems: 78, 74, 70, 58, 54

Problem Extension
How much more did she pay for the 37¢ envelope than she paid for the 20¢ envelope? (*37¢ − 20¢ = 17¢*)

93 TWO-STEP PROBLEM

The post office has old canceled stamps on sale that Wanda has been trying to find. She bought 3 that had the American flag on them. She bought 4 that had pictures on them of presidents of the United States. How many old stamps did Wanda buy?

All old stamps at the post office were on sale for 5¢ each. How much did Wanda pay for the old stamps she bought?

Understanding the Problem
- What does the post office have on sale? (*old canceled stamps*)
- How many stamps did she buy with the American flag? (*3*)
- What pictures were on the other 4 stamps she bought? (*presidents of the United States*)
- How much did each old stamp sell for? (*5¢*)

Solving the Problem
- Which operation can you use to find the total number of old stamps Wanda bought? (*addition*)
- How many did she buy? (*7*)
- Did she pay the same amount for each of the 7 stamps? (*yes*) How much? (*5¢ each*)
- If she paid the same amount for each of the 7 stamps, which operation can you use to find the total amount she paid? (*multiplication*)
- Can you count by 5s and write down the numbers you say?

Solution
Choose the Operations

$3 + 4 = 7 \rightarrow 7 \times 5¢ = 35¢$

Wanda paid 35¢ for the old stamps.

Related Problems: 88, 83

Problem Extension
Suppose the old stamps were on sale for 3¢ each. How much would she have paid for the stamps? (*$7 \times 3¢ = 21¢$*)

94 PROCESS PROBLEM

When Wanda was at the post office, she asked the postal worker if they sold pages for stamp books. The postal worker said they had pages that Wanda could buy. The postal worker said Wanda could buy 2 pages for a total of 5¢. Wanda had 30¢. How many stamp book pages could she buy? Complete the table to help you find out.

Understanding the Problem

- Did the post office have stamp book pages for Wanda to buy? (*yes*)
- How much do they cost? (*2 for 5¢*)
- How much money did Wanda have? (*30¢*)
- What are we trying to find? (*how many pages Wanda could buy with her 30¢*)

Solving the Problem

- What are the numbers in the top row of the table? (*the number of stamp book pages*)
- What are the numbers in the bottom row of the table? (*the cost of that number of pages*)
- How many pages could Wanda buy with 10¢? (*4*)
- Write 15¢ in the next space on the bottom of the table. How many pages could Wanda buy for 15¢? (*6*)
- Do you see a pattern in the top row of numbers? (*multiples of 2*) In the bottom row of numbers? (*multiples of 5*)

Solution

Complete a Table/Look for a Pattern

Number of Stamp Book Pages	2	4	6	8	10	12
Cost	5¢	10¢	15¢	20¢	25¢	30¢

Note: This table has 2 patterns for students to identify—multiples of 2 and multiples of 5.

Wanda could buy 12 pages for 30¢.

Related Problems: 76, 72, 71, 60, 59

Problem Extensions

1. What would it cost Wanda to buy 16 pages? (*40¢*)
2. How many pages could Wanda buy with 50¢? (*20*)

STRATEGY ASSESSMENT IDEAS

Listen and watch as students work to see if they

- place numbers correctly in the table
- use a pattern to correctly extend the table
- interpret the table to arrive at the correct answer

95 PROCESS PROBLEM

On the way home from the visit to the post office, Wanda looked at all the different kinds of mailboxes people have in front of their houses. In front of a large apartment building, she saw 5 groups of mailboxes. She counted the mailboxes in each group and said, "I see a pattern." Can you find the pattern that Wanda found to tell how many mailboxes were in the last group?

MATERIALS

cubes or counters (at least 25 per pair)

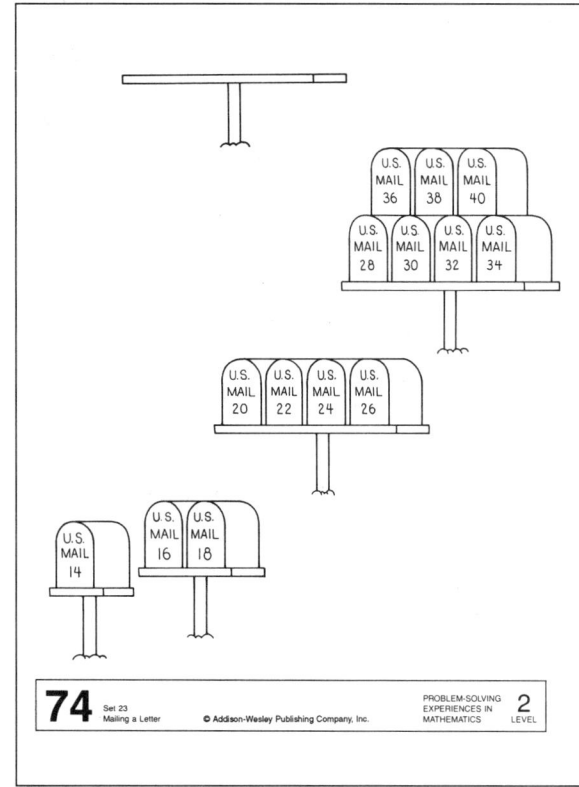

Understanding the Problem

- What did Wanda look at on the way home from the post office? (*the different kinds of mailboxes people have*)
- What did she see in front of a large apartment building? (*5 groups of mailboxes*)
- How many groups of mailboxes are shown on your paper? (*4*)
- How many mailboxes are on the first pole? (*1*) The second pole? (*2*) The third pole? (*4*) The fourth pole? (*7*)
- What are we trying to find? (*the number of boxes on the pole*)

Solving the Problem

Look for a Pattern

- Write the number of mailboxes on each pole at the top of each group of mailboxes. Do you see a pattern in the numbers?
- How many more boxes are in the second group than are in the first group? (*2 – 1 = 1 more*) How many more are in the third group than the second group? (*4 – 2 = 2 more*) The fourth group compared to the third group? (*7 – 4 = 3 more*) Do you see a pattern in the way the number of boxes increases? (*the difference in the number of boxes increases by 1 each time*)

STRATEGY ASSESSMENT IDEAS

Listen and watch as students work to see if they

- describe a pattern formed by the mailboxes
- extend the pattern correctly
- use the pattern to arrive at the correct answer

140

Use Manipulatives

- Make a chart similar to the one shown using the blocks. For each group of mailboxes, make a row on the chart.
- Find the difference between row 1 and 2. What is the difference between row 2 and 3? 3 and 4? 4 and 5?
- What happens to the difference each time? (*it increases by 1*) Do you see a pattern?

Solution

+1 +2 +3 +4

1   2   4   7   (11)

There were 11 mailboxes in the last group.

Related Problems: 94, 76, 72, 71, 60

Problem Extension

What numbers would be on the 11 mailboxes in the fifth group? (*42, 44, 46, 48, 50, 52, 54, 56, 58, 60, 62*)

SET 24

Detective Donna

Donna Shah looks and acts like any 9-year-old, but Donna has a special talent. If anyone in her neighborhood loses a cat or a dog, Donna always seems to be able to find it. Because Donna is so good at finding lost pets, all the people in her neighborhood have started to call her "Detective Donna."

Detective Donna lives in a big neighborhood, and lots of cats and dogs live there. Hardly a week goes by that Donna isn't called and asked to help find a lost pet.

Donna really likes animals. She wants to be a veterinarian when she grows up. Finding lost pets always makes Donna very happy, and she thinks it makes the pets happy too! Animals certainly seem to calm down once Donna finds them. And Donna can tell from the pet owners' smiling faces how glad they are to see their pets again.

Discussion Questions

1. What nickname have the people in Donna Shah's neighborhood given her? (*Detective Donna*)
2. Why is Donna Shah called Detective Donna? (*she helps find lost pets*)
3. What does Donna want to be when she grows up? (*a veterinarian*) What is a veterinarian?
4. Who is happy when Detective Donna finds a lost pet? (*the pet owners*)
5. Would you be a good detective? Why? What would you be good at finding?

96 SKILL ACTIVITY

Tell Missing Data

Problem A
The longest Detective Donna has ever had to look for a lost dog was 6 hours. So far, she can't find Rudy, the German shepherd. How many more hours does she have before she reaches her longest time?

Problem B
Last month, Detective Donna helped find 9 lost cats and dogs. This month she has helped find many more than this. How many more cats and dogs has Donna helped to find this month?

TEACHING ACTIONS

1. Read Problem A to the students. Ask, "Can you solve this problem?"
2. Discuss what information they need to know to solve this problem.
3. (*optional*) Have students make up reasonable data for the problem.
4. (*optional*) Have students solve the problem.
5. Repeat for Problem B.

97 ONE-STEP PROBLEM

On Sunday afternoon, after she did her homework for school the next day, Detective Donna looked for two missing dogs. One dog was easy to find, and it only took Donna about 5 minutes to find it. The other dog ran far away and it took Donna about 45 minutes to find it. How much time did Donna spend altogether on Sunday looking for the two lost dogs?

Understanding the Problem

- What did Donna do on Sunday after she finished her homework? (*looked for 2 missing dogs*)
- Were both dogs easy to find? (*no, only one was easy to find*)
- How long did it take to find the dog that was easy to find? (*5 min.*) The dog that was difficult to find? (*45 min.*)
- What are we trying to find? (*how long Donna spent looking for the 2 dogs*)

Solving the Problem

- If you spend 3 minutes brushing your teeth and 7 minutes combing your hair, how long does it take you to do both? (*10 minutes*) Which operation did you use to find the answer? (*addition*)
- Are you trying to compare the two times? (*no*)
- To find the total amount of time, which operation should you use? (*addition*)

Solution

Choose the Operation

45 + 5 = 50 minutes   or   45
                               + 5
                               ―――
                               50 minutes

Donna spent 50 minutes looking for the 2 dogs.

Related Problems: 92, 78, 74, 70, 58

Problem Extensions

1. How much longer did it take Donna to find the dog that ran far away? (*45 − 5 = 40 minutes*)
2. Suppose it took Donna 45 minutes to find each dog. How long did she spend looking for both? (*45 + 45 = 90 minutes*)

98 TWO-STEP PROBLEM

Last month Detective Donna was asked to help find 4 lost cats and 5 lost dogs. How many cats and dogs was Detective Donna asked to help find last month?

Every time she found a lost dog or cat, Donna gave it a "pet treat." Pet treats cost 3¢ for one piece. If she found all of the cats and dogs she was asked to help find last month, how much did she spend for pet treats?

Understanding the Problem
- How many dogs and cats was Detective Donna asked to help find last month? (*4 cats and 5 dogs*)
- When Donna finds a lost pet, what does she give it? (*1 pet treat*)
- How much do pet treats cost? (*3¢ for 1 piece*)
- What do we want to find? (*how many dogs and cats she was asked to find, and how much she spent for pet treats*)

Solving the Problem
- What is the total number of dogs and cats Donna helped find last month? (*4 + 5 = 9*)
- Which operation do you use to find the total amount of money she spent for pet treats if she spent the same amount for each piece? (*multiplication*)
- Count by 3s and write each number down.

Solution
Choose the Operations

4 + 5 = 9   →   9 × 3¢ = 27¢

Donna spent 27¢ for pet treats.

Related Problems: 93, 88, 83

Problem Extension
Suppose the pet treats cost 5¢ each. How much would she have spent for pet treats? (*9 × 5¢ = 45¢*)

99 PROCESS PROBLEM

Detective Donna was out looking for a lost cat named Karl when she saw a boy fishing. Donna asked the boy if he had seen Karl. The boy said that he had seen a cat down by the river. When Donna asked where, the boy said, "Well, let's see. I think I saw that cat between the big rock and the horse. But when I was walking from the big rock to the horse, it wasn't between the boat and the horse. That's all I remember." Can you use these clues to help Donna tell where she might look for Karl?

Understanding the Problem

- What was Donna looking for? (*a lost cat named Karl*)
- Donna asked somebody if he had seen Karl. Who was it? (*a boy who was fishing*)
- Did the boy think he had seen Karl? (*yes*)
- Between what two things did the boy remember seeing the cat? (*between the rock and the horse*) Can you find the rock and the horse on your paper?
- Between what two things did the boy remember not seeing the cat? (*the boat and the horse*)

Solving the Problem

- Can you show on your picture where the boat has to be? (*see solution*)
- If the boy walked from the rock to the horse and saw a boat, can you draw a boat where it should be? (*see solution*)

Solution

Draw a Picture

The cat should be between the rock and the boat.

Related Problems: 85, 84, 75, 63, 52

Problem Extension

Suppose the boy remembered that the cat wasn't between the big rock and boat. Where was the cat? (*between the boat and the horse*)

STRATEGY ASSESSMENT IDEAS

Listen and watch as students work to see if they

- draw an appropriate picture to solve the problem
- use the picture appropriately to solve the problem
- give an appropriate reason for the picture they chose to draw

147

100 PROCESS PROBLEM

Detective Donna received a secret message about Sparty, a missing poodle. Here's what the note said:

"I think I saw a dog accidentally locked in a room at the Shady Grove Motel. I don't remember the exact room number, but I do remember 3 pieces of information that might help. (1) The room number was greater than 6; (2) the room number was less than 9; and (3) you say the number if you count by 2s beginning at 2. Good luck—I hope this is the dog."

Which room should Detective Donna check?

MATERIALS

number tiles 1–12, paper squares numbered 1–12, 2-color counters, or dark and light counters (12 per group)

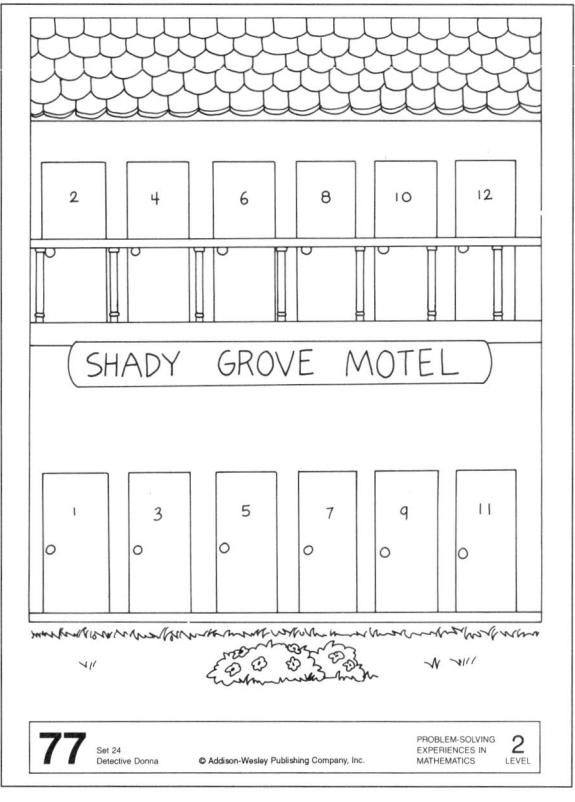

Understanding the Problem

- What did Donna receive a secret message about? (*a missing poodle named Sparty*)
- Where did the message say the dog was? (*accidentally locked in a room*)

Solving the Problem

Use Logical Reasoning

- The room number where the dog was located was greater than what number? (*6*) Using this clue, which rooms could the dog be in? (*7–12*) The room number was less than what number? (*9*) Using this clue, which rooms could the dog be in? (*1–8*)
- When you count by what number will you say the room number? (*2s*)

Use Manipulatives

- Use the number tiles to represent the doors of Shady Grove Motel. Turn over tiles when you are sure they are not the correct answer. (Or, turn 2-color counters from yellow to red; or, replace a dark counter with a light one.)
- If the room number is greater than 6, which tiles can be turned over? (*6 and less than 6*)
- If the room number is less than 9, can we turn over any other tiles? (*yes, 9 and numbers greater than 9*)
- Can any of these numbers left be the number in the clue? (*yes, 8*) Why? (*only 7 and 8 are left and 7 is not an even number*)

STRATEGY ASSESSMENT IDEAS

Listen and watch as students work to see if they

- use a plan to eliminate rooms
- correctly use all conditions given in the problem
- arrive at correct conclusions through reasoning

Solution

Use Logical Reasoning

~~1~~ ~~2~~ ~~3~~ ~~4~~ ~~5~~ ~~6~~ 7 ⑧ ~~9~~ ~~10~~ ~~11~~ ~~12~~

The dog was in room 8.

Related Problems: 99, 90, 85, 84, 75

Problem Extensions

1. Suppose the dog were in a room number that was greater than 6, and you say the room number when you count by 5s. Where was the dog? (*in room 10*)

2. What if the room number were greater than 2 and less than 5. The number was also the sum of two odd numbers. Where was the dog? (*in room 4*)

All Kinds of Trains

Nickie was 8 years old and she liked trains. In fact, she loved them. The very first time Nickie rode on a train she was only 5 years old. She rode with her mom to visit her grandma and grandpa.

The night before Nickie went on the train to visit her grandparents, she had a scary dream. In her dream the train had to cross a big river, but the train tracks didn't have anything to hold them up. Instead, the tracks swayed back and forth like a swing. In the dream she was afraid the train would fall into the river, but just as the train was about to fall in, Nickie's mom woke her up. "It's time to get up, Nickie. We have a big day ahead of us," Mom said.

As you would expect, Nickie was a little nervous when they really did get on the train. When she told her mom about her scary dream, her mom said, "Don't worry, I've crossed that river many times on the train. There is a bridge, but it is solid and very sturdy." From that point on Nickie enjoyed the trip very much.

The next time Nickie took a trip on a train, she was 2 years older (that's right; she was 7). This was a very special train because the engine that pulled the cars was an old-fashioned steam engine. Nickie's dad took her up to the engine compartment so she could see the coal being shoveled into the firebox. The best part of all came when the engineer let her pull the cord to blow the steam whistle. Nickie decided that when she grew up she would be an engineer of a train. She said, "I'm also going to be an artist and a doctor, but only when I'm not driving my train."

Discussion Questions

1. How old was Nickie when she took her first train ride? (*5*)
2. Where did she go on her first train trip? (*to visit her grandma and grandpa*)
3. What happened to Nickie the night before her first train trip? (*she had a scary dream*)
4. What scary thing happened in her dream? (*the train tracks swayed*)
5. Did the train fall into the river in her dream? (*no*)
6. Was Nickie nervous when they really did get on the train? (*yes*)
7. When was the next time Nickie took a train trip? (*2 years later, when she was 7*)
8. What was special about this train? (*it was an old-fashioned steam engine*)
9. What fun thing did Nickie get to do? (*pull the cord to blow the steam whistle*)
10. Have you ever been for a trip on a train?

101 SKILL ACTIVITY

Tell a Story Problem for an Addition Number Sentence

Setting

Nickie and her parents are in their car waiting for a long train to pass by them.

Number Sentence A

30 + 15 = ?

Possible Story Problem for Number Sentence A

Nickie counted 30 red train cars and 15 black train cars. How many red and black cars did she count in all?

Number Sentence B

12 + 9 = ?

Possible Story Problem for Number Sentence B

Twelve cars were lined up on one side of the train track waiting for the train to pass. Nine cars were lined up on the other side of the train track. How many cars were lined up waiting for the train to pass?

Note: Several story problems are possible. Be sure the story problems students make up follow the setting and include both the numbers and the correct operation (addition).

TEACHING ACTIONS

1. Read the story setting.
2. Have students tell a story problem that can be solved using Number Sentence A.
3. Repeat for Number Sentence B.
4. (*optional*) Have students solve both of their story problems.

102 ONE-STEP PROBLEM

Nickie counted 24 people in the dining car on the train she and her mother rode. She counted 8 people in the lounge car. How many more people were in the dining car than in the lounge car?

Understanding the Problem

- What is a dining car? (*a special train car where people go to eat*)
- How many people did Nickie count in the dining car? (*24*)
- What is a lounge car? (*a special car where people sit and read and talk*)
- How many people did Nickie count in the lounge car? (*8*)

Solving the Problem

- Are we trying to find how many people there were altogether? (*no*)
- If she counted 4 people in the dining car and 3 people in the lounge car, how many more people were in the dining car than in the lounge car? (*1*)
- Do you use addition or subtraction to solve this problem? (*subtraction*)
- Can you write a number sentence for this story? (*see solution*)

Solution

Choose the Operation

$24 - 8 = 16$ or $\begin{array}{r} 24 \\ -8 \\ \hline 16 \end{array}$ (*Note:* A trade is involved.)

Nickie counted 16 more people in the dining car than in the lounge car.

Related Problems: 87, 82, 66, 62, 50

Problem Extensions

1. During the train ride, Nickie saw 22 cows grazing in the fields. She also saw 9 horses grazing. How many more cows did she see than horses? (*13*)
2. Nicki got hungry during the train trip, so she ate some peanuts. Before she ate them, she counted how many she had. She had 26 in all. She ate only 8. Now how many peanuts did she have? (*18*)

103 TWO-STEP PROBLEM

Last spring Nickie went to the zoo. Most people go to see the animals, but Nickie went to ride on the train that travels around the zoo. Nickie took 3 rides on the train in the morning and 5 rides in the afternoon. What was the total number of rides Nickie took?

Each ride costs 4 tickets. How many tickets did Nickie need for all the train rides she went on?

Understanding the Problem

- What did Nickie like to go to the zoo to do? (*to ride on the train*)
- How many rides did she go on in the morning? (*3*) In the afternoon? (*5*)
- How much did each ride cost? (*4 tickets*)

Solving the Problem

- What is the first thing you need to find? (*how many total rides she took*)
- Do you use addition or subtraction to find how many total rides she took? (*addition*)
- Did Nickie pay the same amount for each ride? (*yes*) How much? (*4 tickets*)
- If she paid 4 tickets for one ride, how much did she pay for two rides? (*8 tickets*) Three rides? (*12 tickets*)
- Which operation can you use to find the total amount she paid? (*addition or multiplication*)
- Can you write a number sentence to show how much she paid for all the rides? (*see solution*)

Solution

Choose the Operations

Addition and Addition or Addition and Multiplication

$3 + 5 = 8$ or $\begin{array}{r} 3 \\ + 5 \\ \hline 8 \end{array}$

Nickie took 8 rides in all.

4 tickets + 4 tickets + 4 tickets + 4 tickets + 4 tickets + 4 tickets + 4 tickets + 4 tickets = 32 tickets

or

8×4 tickets = 32 tickets

Nickie paid 32 tickets for 8 rides.

Related Problems: 98, 93, 88, 83

Problem Extension

Suppose each ride Nickie took cost 5 tickets. Now how much would she have to pay for all the rides? (*8×5 tickets = 40 tickets*)

104 PROCESS PROBLEM

There are two train stations (called *depots*) at the zoo. When you buy a ticket for a ride, you leave from Depot 1 and get off at Depot 2. There are 6 different ways you can get from Depot 1 to Depot 2 on the train. Two ways are shown on your page. Can you list the other 4?

Understanding the Problem

- What is another name for a train station? (*depot*)
- When you ride on the train, from which depot do you leave? (*Depot 1*)
- When you ride on the train, at which depot do you get off? (*Depot 2*)
- How many different ways are there to go from Depot 1 to Depot 2? (*6 ways*)

Solving the Problem

- Show me track A. Can you run your finger over track A? Can you show me where the train would go if it went on track A and then on track D?
- If the train went on track B first, which track could it go on second? (*D or E*) Are there other ways? Write them down.
- If the train went on track C first, which track could it go on second? (*D or E*) Are there other ways? Write them down.
- Do you have all 6 ways? Have you written them down?

Solution

Complete an Organized List/Use a Picture

| First A then D | First B then D | First C then D |
| First A then E | First B then E | First C then E |

Note: The 6 ways do not have to be written down in this order, but point out that it helps to be organized to be sure you find all the ways.

Related Problems: 100, 90, 89, 85, 84

Problem Extensions

1. Suppose there were 4 different train tracks leaving Depot 1 (A, B, C, and D) and 2 tracks arriving at Depot 2. Now how many different ways could the train go from Depot 1 to Depot 2? (*8*)

2. Suppose there were 3 train tracks from Depot 1 (A, B, and C) and 3 different tracks arriving at Depot 2. How many different ways could the train go from Depot 1 to Depot 2? (*9*)

STRATEGY ASSESSMENT IDEAS

Listen and watch as students work to see if they

- create correct entries for their lists
- organize entries in their lists
- list all possibilities

105 PROCESS PROBLEM

Nickie bought 2 new train cars for her model train set. The 2 cars cost her a total of $28. Which 2 cars did she buy? (Use the picture.)

Understanding the Problem

- How many new cars did Nickie buy for her model train set? (*2*)
- How much did the 2 cars cost? (*$28*)
- Did each car cost $28? (*no, the 2 cars together cost $28*)
- Look at the picture. How much does a steam engine cost? (*$16*)
- Which car costs $8? Point to it.

Solving the Problem

- How many cars did Nickie buy? (*2*) Can you make a guess at which 2 cars she bought? Can you check to see if you are right?
- Could one of the cars be the steam engine? (*no*) Why not?
- Could one of the cars be the $8 car? (*no*) Why not? Which cars are left to choose? (*$13, $15, and $9 cars*)
- If one car cost $13, how much did the other car cost? (*$15*)

Solution

Guess and Check

Several possibilities exist. Two are shown here.

Method 1

Guess $16 + $9 = $25   (*not enough*)
Guess $16 + $13 = $29   (*too much, but close*)
Guess $15 + $13 = $28   (*correct*)

STRATEGY ASSESSMENT IDEAS

Listen and watch as students work to see if they

- make a reasonable first guess (students should choose 2 different train cars)
- make a second guess using what they learn from checking their first guess
- check their answers to be sure all the information was used

Method 2
Try $16 with each other amount.
$16 + $8 = $24
$16 + $13 = $29
$16 + $15 = $31   *(none of these is right)*
$16 + $9 = $25
   Can't be $16.

Try $8 with the remaining cars.
$8 + $13 = $21
$8 + $15 + $23   *(none of these is right)*
$8 + $9 = $17
   Can't be $8.

Try $13 with the remaining cars.
$13 + $9 = $22
$13 + $15 = $28   *(this is it)*

The 2 cars were the $13 and the $15 cars. Is there any other possibility? The only cars left are $15 + $9 = $24. *(no, too low)* The only choices are the $13 car and the $15 car.

Related Problems: 90, 80, 68, 56, 32

Problem Extension
Suppose Nickie bought 3 cars and spent $32. Which 3 cars did she buy? *(the $9 car, the $8 car, and the $15 car)*

SET 26

A Dog's Life

Zeke the hound dog seemed very unhappy. Rita, Zeke's owner, hadn't paid any attention to him for days. Rita's cat, Taco, had just had 5 kittens. Whenever Zeke got close to the kittens, Taco would hiss and Rita would scold Zeke and tell him to go away.

One day, Zeke ran away from home. It was a hot summer day, and it didn't take long before Zeke was thirsty, tired, and hungry. Soon, Zeke stopped and slowly turned around. Suddenly he started running back home as fast as he could go.

By the time Zeke reached home it was dark. Rita was sitting on the front porch with her head in her hands. "Zeke, Zeke, where can you be?" she cried. "You're always home at supper time." Very quietly Zeke walked up to Rita and licked her hand. She looked up quickly. "Zeke, oh Zeke! You're back," she cried. "I'm so glad to see you. Where did you go?" "Arf, Arf," Zeke barked. Rita hugged him tightly.

Discussion Questions

1. Why did Zeke seem unhappy? (*his owner was not paying attention to him*)
2. How many kittens did Taco the cat have? (*5*)
3. What did Zeke do one hot summer day? (*he ran away*)
4. Have you ever had a pet run away? How did it make you feel?
5. What did Zeke do after he stopped and turned around? (*he ran home*)
6. Where was Rita when he reached home? (*on the front porch*)
7. Was Rita happy to see Zeke? (*yes*) Do you think Zeke was happy?

106 SKILL ACTIVITY

Tell a Story Problem for a Subtraction Number Sentence

Setting

Zeke the hound dog likes doggie biscuits. Rita just bought a new bag of doggie biscuits for Zeke.

Number Sentence A

11 – 6 = ?

Possible Story Problem for Number Sentence A

Rita put 11 doggie biscuits in Zeke's dish and went out of the room. When she returned, Zeke had eaten 6. How many doggie biscuits were still in the dish?

Number Sentence B

23 – 17 = ?

Possible Story Problem for Number Sentence B

On Monday Zeke ate 23 doggie biscuits. On Tuesday he ate 17 doggie biscuits. How many more doggie biscuits did Zeke eat on Monday than on Tuesday?

TEACHING ACTIONS

1. Read the story setting.
2. Have students tell a story problem that can be solved using Number Sentence A.
3. Repeat for Number Sentence B.
4. (*optional*) Have students solve both of their story problems.

107 ONE-STEP PROBLEM

Zeke likes to bury bones in secret places in back of the house. One month Zeke buried 15 bones. The next month he buried 17 bones. How many bones did he bury in the 2 months?

Understanding the Problem

- Where does Zeke like to bury bones? (*in secret places in back of the house*)
- How many bones did Zeke bury the first month? (*15*) How many the second month? (*17*)

Solving the Problem

- Are you being asked to find how many bones he buried altogether? (*yes*)
- What operation do you use when you put together 2 sets? (*addition*)
- Can you write a number sentence to solve this problem? (*see solution*)

Solution

Choose the Operation

$15 + 17 = 32$ or $\begin{array}{r} 15 \\ + 17 \\ \hline 32 \end{array}$

Zeke buried 32 bones in 2 months.

Related Problems: 97, 92, 78, 74, 70

Problem Extension

Suppose Zeke buried 15 bones one month, 12 bones the next month, and 11 bones the third month. How many bones did Zeke bury in the 3 months? (*this is a 2-step problem: 15 + 12 = 27, 27 + 11 = 38*)

108 TWO-STEP PROBLEM

Zeke buried 11 bones near the apple tree in back of the house. He also buried 15 bones near the rose bush. One day when Rita forgot to feed him, he dug up 9 bones and had a real feast. How many bones does Zeke still have buried?

Understanding the Problem

- How many bones did Zeke bury near the apple tree? (*11*)
- How many bones did he bury near the rose bush? (*15*)
- Why did Zeke dig up some of his bones? (*Rita forgot to feed him and he was hungry*)
- How many bones did he dig up? (*9*)

Solving the Problem

- What is the first thing you need to find? (*how many bones he buried in all*)
- How can you find the total number of bones he buried? (*add 11 and 15*)
- How many bones did Zeke bury? (*11 + 15 = 26 bones*)
- If he buried 26 bones and dug up 9, which operation would you use to find out how many bones are still buried? (*subtraction*)
- Can you write a subtraction sentence to show how many bones are still buried? (*26 − 9 = 17 bones*)

Solution

Choose the Operations

Step 1: 11 + 15 = 26   or   11
                                 + 15

                                  26

Zeke buried 26 bones.

Step 2: 26 − 9 = 17   or   26
                                − 9

                                 17

Zeke still has 17 bones buried.

Related Problems: 108, 98, 93, 88, 83

Problem Extension

One day Zeke buried 13 bones, and the next day he buried 9 bones. On the third day he buried 7 old tennis balls. How many more bones did he bury than tennis balls?
(*13 + 9 = 22, 22 − 7 = 15*)

109 > PROCESS PROBLEM

Rita was so happy that Zeke had come home that she went to the pet store to buy him a special treat. Rita knows that Zeke loves dog yummies. Dog yummies come in packs of 2 for 6¢. Rita has 33¢ to spend on dog yummies. How many dog yummies can she buy?

MATERIALS
cubes (14 per pair); pennies or counters (42 per pair)

Understanding the Problem

- Why did Rita go to the pet store? (*to buy Zeke a special treat*)
- What treat does Zeke love? (*dog yummies*)
- Can you buy just one dog yummy? (*no, they come in packs of 2*)
- How much do 2 dog yummies cost? (*6¢*)
- How much money does Rita have to spend on dog yummies? (*33¢*)

Solving the Problem

Complete a Table/Look for a Pattern

- Look at the table. How much do 2 dog yummies cost? (*6¢*) How much do 4 dog yummies cost? (*12¢*) Do you see a pattern in the top row? (*multiples of 2*) What number comes after 2 and 4? (*6*) Can you complete the top row?
- What do the numbers in the bottom row show? (*the cost of dog yummies*)
- How much more is 12¢ than 6¢? (*6¢*) What number comes after 12¢? (*18¢*) Can you see a pattern to help you complete the bottom row? (*multiples of 6*)

Use Manipulatives

- Use cubes to represent the dog yummies. If you bought 2 dog yummies, how much would it cost? (*6¢*)
- Has Rita spent 33¢ yet? (*no*) How much would 4 dog yummies cost? (*12¢*) What pattern do you see? (*6¢ more for every 2 more dog yummies*)
- Complete the table using this information.

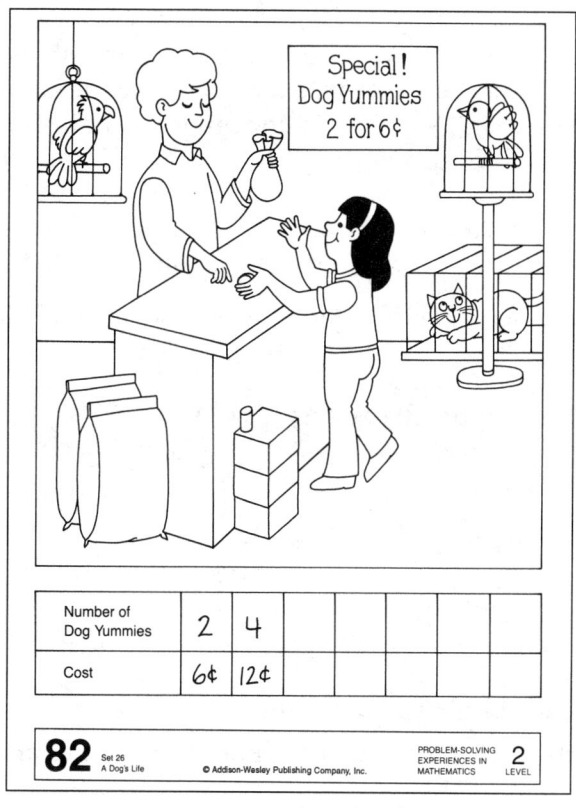

Solution

Complete a Table/Look for a Pattern

Number of Dog Yummies	2	4	6	8	10	12	14
Cost	6¢	12¢	18¢	24¢	30¢	36¢	

↑

Rita can buy 10 dog yummies and have 3¢ left over.

Related Problems: 95, 94, 76, 72, 71

STRATEGY ASSESSMENT IDEAS

Listen and watch as students work to see if they

- place cubes and pennies correctly in the table
- use a pattern to correctly extend the table
- interpret the table to arrive at the correct answer

Problem Extensions

1. What would it cost Rita to buy 14 dog yummies? (*42¢*)
2. How many dog yummies can she buy with 48¢? (*16*)

110 PROCESS PROBLEM

Rita wrote a story about Zeke the hound dog and Taco the cat. In her story, Zeke dug up all his bones to find out how many he had. Taco the cat said, "Zeke, you aren't even smart enough to count how many you have." Zeke answered, "Oh yeah? Not only do I know how many bones I have, but I have also put them into nice neat piles. The piles make a pattern. Can you figure how many bones are in the last pile?"

(*Optional question:* How many bones does Zeke have in all?)

Understanding the Problem

- In Rita's story, why did Zeke dig up all his bones? (*to find out how many he had*)
- Did Taco think Zeke could count? (*no, she didn't think he was smart enough*)
- What did Zeke do with his bones after he dug them up? (*put them in piles in a pattern*)

Solving the Problem

- Can you write down how many bones are in each pile? (*1, 3, 6, 10*)
- Do you see a pattern? 3 is how much more than 1? (*2*) 6 is how much more than 3? (*3*) 10 is how much more than 6? (*4*)
- How many bones are in the fourth pile? (*see solution*)

Solution

Look for a Pattern

2 more 3 more 4 more 5 more

1   3   6   10   15

There are 15 bones in the last pile.

(*Optional:* 1 + 3 + 6 + 10 + 15 = 35; Zeke had 35 bones.)

Related Problems: 109, 95, 94, 76, 72

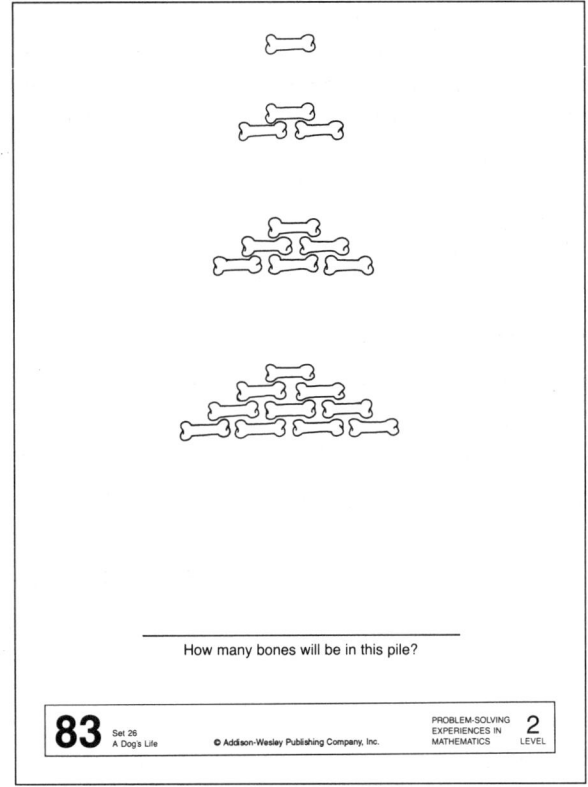

How many bones will be in this pile?

Problem Extension

In Rita's story, suppose that Zeke remembered he had more bones buried. He dug them up and put them in a neat pile. To his surprise, they followed the same pattern as the other piles. In fact, the pile was next in the pattern. How many bones were in the next pile? (*6 more than 15, or 21 bones*)

STRATEGY ASSESSMENT IDEAS

Listen and watch as students work to see if they

- describe a pattern formed by the piles of bones
- extend the pattern correctly
- use the pattern to arrive at the correct answer

Ralph the Superchicken

Kenny Lee is a boy who lives in a very big city. He thinks that someday he would like to live in the country and raise animals. Kenny also likes to write stories—mostly stories about a character he named Ralph the Superchicken!

Ralph the Superchicken lives in a small town in the country called Cornyopolis. Kenny calls Ralph a Superchicken because he is very fast and strong (for a chicken at least), and because he helps people in his home town when they are in trouble.

Why, just yesterday Kenny wrote a story in which Ralph helped Farmer Ferdinand find 4 cows that ran away during the night. Last week, Ralph saved another farmer's chickens by scaring away a big red fox from the chicken coop. Ralph the Superchicken isn't afraid of anything!

When Ralph isn't needed to do super things, he looks just like a regular chicken. In fact, most people and other chickens don't even know Ralph is really Ralph the Superchicken unless he's wearing one of his special Ralph the Superchicken shirts.

Discussion Questions

1. Who writes stories about Ralph the Superchicken? (*Kenny Lee*)
2. Do you remember the name of the town where Ralph the Superchicken lives? (*Cornyopolis*)
3. Why does Kenny call Ralph a Superchicken? (*because he is very fast and strong and because he helps people*)
4. What kinds of things might Ralph do to help people in his home town?
5. What does Ralph wear so people know he is Ralph the Superchicken? (*a special shirt*)

111 SKILL ACTIVITY

Tell a Story Problem

Setting

Ralph the Superchicken is so strong that he can lift other chickens with his feet.

Number Sentence A

40 + 25 = ?

Possible Story Problem for Number Sentence A

One day Ralph wanted to show off how strong he was. He held 40 chickens up in the air with one foot and 25 chickens up in the air with the other foot. Altogether, how many chickens did Ralph hold?

Number Sentence B

8 + 14 = ?

Possible Story Problem for Number Sentence B

Ralph's friend, Ned, thought he was a Superchicken too. He tried holding 8 chickens with one foot and 14 with the other, but they all fell down. How many chickens did Ned try to hold?

TEACHING ACTIONS

1. Read the story setting.
2. Have students tell a story problem that would be solved using Number Sentence A.
3. Repeat for Number Sentence B.
4. (*optional*) Have students solve their story problems.

112 ONE-STEP PROBLEM

It takes a regular chicken 35 minutes to run from the chicken coop to the pond and back. Ralph the Superchicken can run from the chicken coop to the pond and back in only 18 minutes. How many minutes longer does it take a regular chicken to run to the pond and back than it takes Ralph?

Understanding the Problem
- How long does it take a regular chicken to run from the chicken coop to the pond and back? (*35 minutes*)
- Does Ralph, the Superchicken, run faster or slower than regular chickens? (*faster*)
- How long does it take Ralph to run from the chicken coop to the pond and back? (*18 minutes*)

Solving the Problem
- Are you trying to find the total amount of time in the problem? (*no*)
- If your friend took 5 minutes to run around the block and you only took 3 minutes to run around the block, how much longer did it take your friend? (*5 – 3 = 2 minutes*) Which operation did you use to find that answer? (*subtraction*)
- Which operation do you use to compare 2 numbers to find how much greater 1 is than the other? (*subtraction*)

Solution
Choose the Operation

35 – 18 = 17   or   35
                      – 18
                      ____
                        17

It takes a regular chicken 17 minutes longer than it takes Ralph the Superchicken.

Related Problems: 102, 87, 82, 66, 62

Problem Extensions
1. How long would it take Ralph to run two times from the chicken coop to the pond and back if each trip took 18 minutes? (*18 + 18 = 36 minutes*)
2. If a complete trip takes Ralph 18 minutes, how long does it take Ralph to run from the chicken coop to the pond? (*9 minutes*)

113 ▶ TWO-STEP PROBLEM

Ralph the Superchicken helps Farmer Ferdinand round up his cows every night and walk them into the barn. Farmer Ferdinand has 10 brown cows and 24 black cows. Yesterday, Ralph and Farmer Ferdinand went out to the barn to give the cows some water, and there were only 21 cows in the barn. How many cows did Ralph and Farmer Ferdinand have to round up again?

Understanding the Problem

- What does Ralph help Farmer Ferdinand do every night? (*round up his cows and walk them to the barn*)
- What does it mean to "round up" cows?
- What colors are Farmer Ferdinand's cows? (*brown and black*)
- How many brown cows does he have? (*10*) Black cows? (*24*)
- How many cows were in the barn when they checked? (*21*)
- Were all of the cows in the barn? (*no*)
- What are we trying to find? (*how many cows got out of the barn and had to be brought back*)

Solving the Problem

- How can you find the total number of cows Farmer Ferdinand has? (*add*) How many cows hoes he have? (*10 + 24 = 34*)
- If he has 34 cows altogether and only 21 were in the barn, which operation would you use to find how many ran away? (*subtraction*) How many ran away? (*34 − 21 = 13*)

Solution

Choose the Operations

10 + 24 = 34   →   34 − 21 = 13

Thirteen cows had to be rounded up and put back in the barn.

Related Problems: 108, 103, 98, 93, 88

Problem Extension

Suppose there were only 18 cows in the barn. How many got out? (*34 − 18 = 16*)

114 PROCESS PROBLEM

Ralph the Superchicken has three shirts he can wear when he goes out to help people. One shirt has a circle on the front. Another has a triangle on the front, and another has a square on the front. Inside each shape, there's one letter—either the letter R for "Ralph," C for "chicken," or S for "super." The S is in the shape that has 3 points. The C is not in the shape with 4 sides. Which shapes and letters are on Ralph's shirts?

MATERIALS

circle, square, and triangle attribute blocks; or counters, pattern block squares, and triangles (1 of each shape per group)

Understanding the Problem

- How many different shirts does Ralph have? (*3*)
- Are they all the same? (*no*)
- What shapes are on the shirts? (*one has a circle, one a triangle, and one a square*)
- What is inside each shape? (*a letter*) Which letters? (*an R, a C, or an S*)
- The S is in a shape with how many points? (*3*)
- Where isn't the C? (*in the shape with 4 sides*)

Solving the Problem

Use Logical Reasoning

- If the S is in the shape with 3 sides, which shape is the S in? (*the triangle*) Which shapes are left? (*circle, square*)
- Which shape isn't the C in? (*the square*)
- If the S is in the triangle, can any other letter also be in the triangle? (*no*)
- If the S is in the triangle and C is not in the square, in which shape must the C be? (*the circle*)

Use Manipulatives

- What shape is the S in? (*triangle*) Put aside the shape for the S and record this information. (*triangle = S*)
- Which shapes are left? (*circle and square*) Which one is not C? (*square*) If this shape is not C, what does it have to be? (*R*) Record. (*square = R*)
- Which shape is left? (*circle*) Which letter is left? (*C*) Do these go together? (*yes*)

▶ *turn the page*

STRATEGY ASSESSMENT IDEAS

Listen and watch as students work to see if they

- use a plan to place the blocks on the shirts and to record their work
- correctly use all conditions given in the problem
- arrive at correct conclusions through reasoning

Solution

Draw a Picture/Use Logical Reasoning

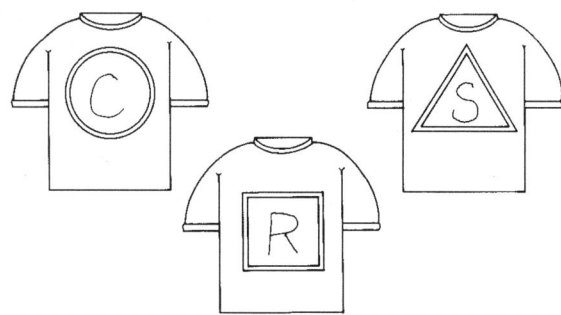

Related Problems: 104, 100, 99, 90, 85

Problem Extension

Using the same story, suppose the C were in the shape with 4 corners. What letters and shapes go together now? (*C = square, S = triangle, R = circle*)

115 PROCESS PROBLEM

Ralph the Superchicken is becoming quite a hero around his home town. Just yesterday, the newspaper in Ralph's home town had a picture of Ralph on the front page and a table showing how many people Ralph has helped during the last 3 months. If the number of people Ralph helps continues to increase the same way, how many people will Ralph help in April, May, and June?

Understanding the Problem

- What does it mean to become a hero?
- What was in the newspaper? (*a picture of Ralph and a table showing how many people Ralph has helped in the last 3 months*)
- How many people did Ralph help in January? (*2*) February? (*5*) March? (*8*)
- What are we trying to find? (*how many people Ralph will help in April, May, and June*)

Solving the Problem

- How many more people did Ralph help in February than he helped in January? (*5 − 2 = 3 more*)
- How many more people did he help in March than he helped in February? (*8 − 5 = 3 more*)
- Do you see a pattern in the number of people Ralph helps each month? (*3 more than the previous month*)

Related Problems: 110, 109, 95, 94, 76

Problem Extension

If this pattern continues, in which month will Ralph help 23 people? (*August*)

Solution

Complete a Table/Look for a Pattern

Month	January	February	March	April	May	June
People Helped	2	5	8	11	14	17

Ralph will help 11 people in April, 14 in May, and 17 in June.

STRATEGY ASSESSMENT IDEAS

Listen and watch as students work to see if they

- place numbers correctly in the table
- use a pattern to correctly extend the table
- interpret the table to arrive at the correct answer

School Carnival

Yung-Su is a second grader at Gateway Elementary School. Yesterday was the annual spring carnival on the playground of Yung-Su's school. Since Yung-Su's father helped all day at the carnival selling tickets for some of the rides, Yung-Su was allowed to stay all day at the carnival too.

The carnival at Yung-Su's school wasn't just a small one with a few rides and a few games. This carnival was a big one! It had a lot of rides, including Yung-Su's favorite rides, the Ferris wheel and the merry-go-round. The carnival also had a lot of games, and at every game you could win a big prize.

Yung-Su had saved her allowance for several weeks getting ready for the carnival. When she arrived at the carnival, she didn't run to the first ride or game she saw like most of the children. Instead, she stopped and looked at all the games and then decided how she wanted to spend her money. She knew she didn't have enough money to ride every ride and play every game, but she did have enough to do everything she really wanted to do. Yung-Su also wanted to be sure to save some money for all the delicious food at the carnival.

Discussion Questions

1. What was held on the playground of Yung-Su's school? (*a carnival*)
2. Why was Yung-Su allowed to stay at the carnival all day? (*her father helped all day selling tickets*)
3. Was the carnival at Yung-Su's school a small one? (*no*) How can you tell? (*it had lots of rides and games*)
4. Where did Yung-Su get her money for the carnival? (*she saved her allowance*)
5. What kinds of rides and games might be at a carnival like the one at Yung-Su's school?
6. What rides and games would you want to try at a carnival?

116 SKILL ACTIVITY

Tell a Story Problem

Setting

Yung-Su's father worked at the carnival selling tickets to the Ferris wheel and tickets to the roller coaster.

Number Sentence A

67 – 23 = ?

Possible Story Problem for Number Sentence A

During the first hour, Yung-Su's father sold 67 roller coaster tickets and 23 Ferris wheel tickets. How many more roller coaster tickets did he sell than Ferris wheel tickets?

Number Sentence B

40 – 28 = ?

Possible Story Problem for Number Sentence B

The roller coaster has enough seats to hold 40 people. So far, only 28 seats are full. How many seats are empty?

TEACHING ACTIONS

1. Read the story setting.
2. Have students tell a story problem that would be solved using Number Sentence A.
3. Repeat for Number Sentence B.
4. (*optional*) Have students solve their story problems.

117 ONE-STEP PROBLEM

On Monday after the school's spring carnival, Yung-Su's teacher told the class that this year's carnival was the largest one ever. They sold tickets to 324 children and 65 adults. How many people bought tickets to this year's carnival?

Understanding the Problem

- What did Yung-Su's teacher tell the class? (*this year's carnival was the largest one ever*)
- How many tickets were sold to children this year? (*324*)
- How many adults bought tickets? (*65*)
- What are we trying to find? (*the total number of people that bought tickets for the carnival*)

Solving the Problem

- If 3 children and 2 adults bought tickets, how many people bought tickets to the carnival? (*3 + 2 = 5*) Which operation did you use to find the answer? (*addition*)
- If you want to find the total number for the 2 groups, which operation should you use? (*addition*)

Solution

Choose the Operation

324 + 65 = 389   or   324
                                           + 65
                                           ―――
                                            389

389 people bought tickets to the carnival.

Related Problems: 107, 97, 92, 78, 74

Problem Extension

Of the 65 adults who bought tickets, 44 were men and 21 were women. How many more men than women bought tickets to the carnival? (*44 − 21 = 23*)

118 TWO-STEP PROBLEM

Tickets for all of the rides at the school's carnival cost 5¢ each. When Yung-Su arrived at the carnival, she bought 3 tickets for the merry-go-round and 5 tickets for the Ferris wheel. How much did Yung-Su spend for the tickets to these rides? 3 tickets for the merry-go-round and 5 tickets for the Ferris wheel. How much did Yung-Su spend for the tickets to these rides?

Understanding the Problem

- How much do ride tickets cost? (*5¢*) Do all ride tickets cost this? (*yes*)
- How many tickets did Yung-Su buy for the merry-go-round? (*3*) The Ferris wheel? (*5*)
- What are we trying to find? (*the total amount of money Yung-Su spent for these rides*)

Solving the Problem

- What is the total number of ride tickets Yung-Su bought for these rides? (*3 + 5 = 8*)
- If each ticket cost the same, which operation can you use to find the total cost for all of the tickets? (*multiplication*)

Solution

Choose the Operations

3 + 5 = 8   →   8 × 5¢ = 40¢

Yung-Su spent a total of 40¢ for ride tickets.

Related Problems: 113, 108, 103, 98, 93

Problem Extension

If ride tickets cost only 3¢ each, how much would Yung-Su have paid for all of the tickets? (*8 × 3¢ = 24¢*)

119 PROCESS PROBLEM

This year at the school's spring carnival, sandwiches and drinks were sold in the school cafeteria. Yung-Su wanted to get one sandwich and one drink for lunch. There were 8 different ways Yung-Su can have one of the sandwiches and one of the drinks. Four of the 8 ways are listed. Can you list the other 4?

MATERIALS

white and orange cubes (4 of each color per group); orange, white, red, and yellow counters (at least 1 of each color per group)

Understanding the Problem

- What was sold in the school cafeteria? (*sandwiches and drinks*)
- What did Yung-Su want for lunch? (*1 sandwich and 1 drink*)
- What sandwiches did Yung-Su have to choose from? (*chicken and cheese*) Drinks? (*orange, milk, apple, lemonade*)
- Could Yung-Su buy 2 drinks for lunch? (*no*)

Solving the Problem

Make an Organized List

- Can you think of a combination that was not listed? For all 4 choices listed on your paper, which sandwich is shown? (*chicken*)
- Can you list the possible lunches with cheese as the sandwich?

Use Manipulatives

- Use the cubes to represent sandwiches, and the counters to represent drinks.
- Use one of your manipulatives to represent each type of sandwich or drink. Place cubes and counters on the combinations that are listed.
- Can you find the 4 combinations that are not listed?

SPRING CARNIVAL TREATS MENU

Sandwiches
chicken
cheese

Drinks
orange
milk
apple
lemonade

chicken – orange drink _____
chicken – milk _____
chicken – apple drink _____
chicken – lemonade _____

88 Set 28 School Carnival

Solution

Make an Organized List

chicken—orange drink   cheese—orange drink
chicken—milk   cheese—milk
chicken—apple drink   cheese—apple drink
chicken—lemonade   cheese—lemonade

Related Problems: 104, 89, 79, 67, 55

Problem Extension

Suppose Yung-Su could also choose a hamburger. Can you list the additional choices Yung-Su has for lunch?

STRATEGY ASSESSMENT IDEAS

Listen and watch as students work to see if they

- create correct entries for their lists
- organize entries in their lists
- list all possibilities

120 PROCESS PROBLEM

Yung-Su played the ball toss game as soon as she arrived at the school spring carnival. For 10¢ you get to throw 3 balls at a board with holes in it. Each hole has a different shape and is worth a different number of points. If you score more than 65 points with the 3 balls, you win a prize. Yung-Su scored 75 points. If she threw a ball into 3 different holes, in which holes did she throw balls to score 75 points?

Understanding the Problem

- What was the name of the game Yung-Su played at the carnival? (*ball toss game*)
- How many balls do you get to throw for 10¢? (*3*)
- How do you play the game? (*throw balls through the holes and add up the points*)
- Is each hole worth the same number of points? (*no*)
- What do you have to do to win a prize? (*score more than 65 points*)
- How many points did Yung-Su score? (*75*)
- Did she throw 2 balls in the same hole? (*no*)

Solving the Problem

- Could Yung-Su have thrown all 3 balls through the hole worth 25 points? (*no, she put the balls in 3 different holes*)
- Can you guess which 3 holes Yung-Su threw the balls in and add to check your guess? (*see solution*)

Solution

Guess and Check
- Try 22 + 20 + 15 = 57 (*too low*)
- Try 20 + 25 + 42 = 87 (*too high*)
- Try 13 + 20 + 42 = 75 (*correct*)

Yung-Su threw the balls in the holes worth 13, 20, and 42 points.

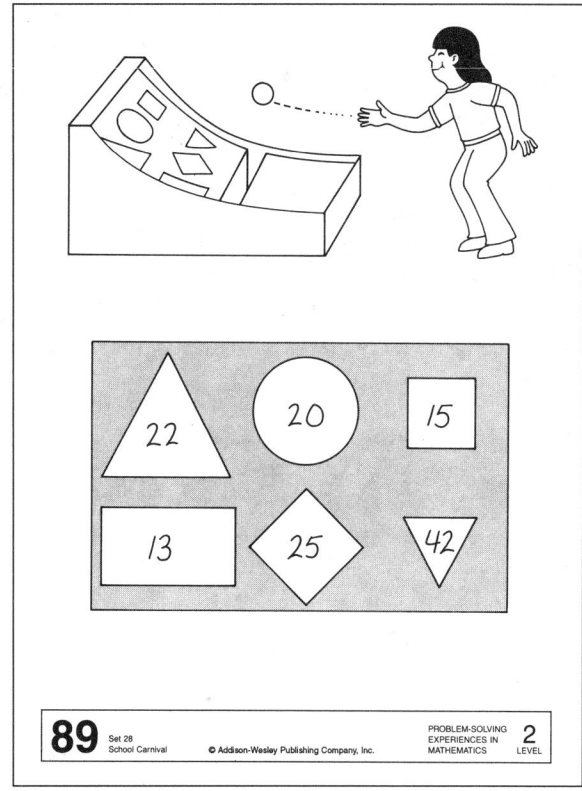

Related Problems: 105, 90, 80, 68, 56

Problem Extension

The next time Yung-Su played the ball toss game, she threw all 3 balls in the same hole and scored 45 points. Which box did Yung-Su throw the balls in? (*15*)

STRATEGY ASSESSMENT IDEAS

Listen and watch as students work to see if they

- make a reasonable first guess (students should choose 3 different numbers)
- make a second guess using what they learn from checking the first guess
- check their answer to be sure that all the information was used

ASSESSMENT APPENDIX

This appendix contains four tools to help you assess your students' progress.

Strategy Implementation Checklist

The Strategy Implementation Checklist contains characteristics of student performance related to each problem-solving strategy. These characteristics can be used to assess student progress over time in their ability to use strategies appropriately. Also, the specific performance characteristics can be used to analyze which aspects of implementing particular strategies students can carry out and which they cannot carry out.

Problem-Solving Observation Checklist

The *Problem-Solving Observation Checklist* includes general problem-solving behaviors and dispositions to be observed and analyzed over time. The first three items address students' selection and use of problem-solving strategies. Item 4 refers to the general approach students use to solve problems, and items 5 and 6 refer to students' dispositions related to solving problems. This checklist can be used as you observe students working in groups solving problems and as you analyze student work on a problem and reflect on their behavior and dispositions.

Focused Holistic Assessment Rubric

The five-level *Focused Holistic Assessment Rubric* is a holistic system for assessing written work, including students' written solutions to problems and, possibly, their written explanations of their problem-solving processes. This assessment method is a *holistic* method because it focuses on the total solution. It is a *focused* method because one number is assigned to a student's work according to specific criteria related to the thinking processes involved in solving problems. To use the rubric, begin by asking whether the student's paper meets any of the criteria listed under *4 Points*. If so, assign that paper 4 points. If not, move on to the *3 Points* category, and so on.

Mathematics Portfolio Profile Checklist

The intended purpose of a portfolio determines its contents and the method used to assess it. One common use of portfolios is as a collection of student work that can be analyzed for growth over time—that is, to give you a profile of the student's growth in mathematics. It is best to use a small number of criteria to develop such a profile. The following three criteria for the evaluation of portfolios are particularly appropriate for the primary grades:

- the ability to engage in problem solving and mathematical reasoning
- the use of oral, written, and visual modes—approaches or methods of doing mathematical activities—to describe mathematical concepts and relations
- the development of healthy dispositions toward mathematics

The *Mathematics Portfolio Profile Checklist* is designed with these three criteria in mind.

Strategy Implementation Checklist

MAKE A TABLE/ LOOK FOR A PATTERN	PLACES ITEMS CORRECTLY IN THE TABLE
	USES A PATTERN TO CORRECTLY EXTEND THE TABLE
	INTERPRETS THE TABLE TO ARRIVE AT THE CORRECT ANSWER
LOOK FOR A PATTERN	DESCRIBES THE PATTERN FORMED BY INFORMATION IN THE PROBLEM
	EXTENDS THE PATTERN CORRECTLY
	USES THE PATTERN TO ARRIVE AT THE ANSWER
DRAW A PICTURE	DRAWS APPROPRIATE PICTURES TO REPRESENT INFORMATION IN THE PROBLEM
	USES PICTURES APPROPRIATELY
	GIVES APPROPRIATE REASONS FOR USING PICTURES
GUESS AND CHECK	MAKES GUESSES THAT INDICATE AN UNDERSTANDING OF THE PROBLEM
	USES PREVIOUS GUESSES TO MAKE BETTER GUESSES
	CHECKS GUESSES USING THE INFORMATION GIVEN IN THE PROBLEM
	GIVES APPROPRIATE REASONS FOR GUESSES
MAKE AN ORGANIZED LIST	CREATES CORRECT ENTRIES FOR A LIST
	ORGANIZES ENTRIES IN THE LIST
	LISTS ALL POSSIBLE ENTRIES
USE LOGICAL REASONING	USES A PLAN FOR RECORDING REASONING
	CORRECTLY USES ALL CONDITIONS GIVEN IN THE PROBLEM
	ARRIVES AT CORRECT CONCLUSIONS THROUGH REASONING

STUDENT

Problem-Solving Observation Checklist

STUDENT _____

DATE _____

	Frequently	**Sometimes**	**Never**
1. Selects appropriate solution strategies.	_____	_____	_____
2. Accurately implements solution strategies.	_____	_____	_____
3. Tries a different solution strategy when stuck (without help from the teacher).	_____	_____	_____
4. Approaches problems in a systematic manner (clarifies the question, identifies needed data, selects and implements a solution strategy, checks solution).	_____	_____	_____
5. Shows a willingness to try problems.	_____	_____	_____
6. Demonstrates self-confidence.	_____	_____	_____

STUDENT _____

DATE _____

	Frequently	**Sometimes**	**Never**
1. Selects appropriate solution strategies.	_____	_____	_____
2. Accurately implements solution strategies.	_____	_____	_____
3. Tries a different solution strategy when stuck (without help from the teacher).	_____	_____	_____
4. Approaches problems in a systematic manner (clarifies the question, identifies needed data, selects and implements a solution strategy, checks solution).	_____	_____	_____
5. Shows a willingness to try problems.	_____	_____	_____
6. Demonstrates self-confidence.	_____	_____	_____

© Addison-Wesley Publishing Company, Inc.

Focused Holistic Assessment Rubric

4 POINTS
These papers have any of the following characteristics:
- The student made an error in carrying out an appropriate solution strategy. However, the error does not reflect misunderstanding of the problem or lack of knowledge of how to implement the strategy, but is a copying or a computational error.
- The student selected and implemented appropriate strategies and gave the correct answer in terms of the data in the problem.

3 POINTS
These papers have any of the following characteristics:
- The student implemented a solution strategy that could have led to the correct solution but misunderstood part of the problem or ignored a condition in the problem.
- The student applied an appropriate solution strategy, but
  a. answered the problem incorrectly for no apparent reason,
  b. gave the correct numerical part of the answer but did not label it or labeled it incorrectly, or
  c. gave no answer
- The student gave the correct answer and apparently selected appropriate solution strategies, but the student's implementation of the strategies is not completely clear.

2 POINTS
These papers have any of the following characteristics:
- The student used an inappropriate strategy and obtained an incorrect answer but showed some understanding of the problem.
- The student applied an appropriate solution strategy, but
  a. did not carry it out far enough to find the solution (e.g., the student made the first 2 entries in an organized list), or
  b. implemented the strategy incorrectly, leading to no answer or to an incorrect answer
- The student successfully reached a subgoal, but could go no farther.
- The student gave the correct answer, but
  a. the work is not understandable, or
  b. no work is shown

1 POINT
These papers have any of the following characteristics:
- The student made a start toward finding the solution—beyond just copying data from the problem—that reflects some understanding of the problem, but the approach used would not have led to a correct solution.
- The student began with an inappropriate strategy and did not carry it out, with no evidence that the student turned to another strategy.
- The student apparently tried to reach a subgoal but never did.

0 POINTS
These papers have any of the following characteristics:
- The student left the paper blank.
- The student simply recopied the data in the problem, but either did nothing with the data or did something that appears to show no understanding of the problem.
- The student gave an incorrect answer and showed no other work.

© Addison-Wesley Publishing Company, Inc.

Mathematics Portfolio Profile Checklist

STUDENT _____	Substantial Growth	Some Growth	No Growth

PROBLEM SOLVING AND REASONING

	Substantial Growth	Some Growth	No Growth
1. Understands information given in problems	_____	_____	_____
2. Applies strategies to solve problems	_____	_____	_____
3. Draws logical conclusions and gives reasons for them	_____	_____	_____

ORAL, WRITTEN, AND VISUAL MODES

	Substantial Growth	Some Growth	No Growth
1. Relates manipulatives, pictures, and diagrams to mathematical ideas and situations	_____	_____	_____
2. Relates everyday languages to mathematical language and symbols	_____	_____	_____

MATHEMATICAL DISPOSITION

	Substantial Growth	Some Growth	No Growth
1. Has confidence in ability to do mathematics	_____	_____	_____
2. Takes risks exploring mathematical ideas and trying alternatives	_____	_____	_____
3. Perseveres in mathematics activities	_____	_____	_____
4. Is interested in doing mathematics	_____	_____	_____

STUDENT _____ | Substantial Growth | Some Growth | No Growth

PROBLEM SOLVING AND REASONING

	Substantial Growth	Some Growth	No Growth
1. Understands information given in problems	_____	_____	_____
2. Applies strategies to solve problems	_____	_____	_____
3. Draws logical conclusions and gives reasons for them	_____	_____	_____

ORAL, WRITTEN, AND VISUAL MODES

	Substantial Growth	Some Growth	No Growth
1. Relates manipulatives, pictures, and diagrams to mathematical ideas and situations	_____	_____	_____
2. Relates everyday languages to mathematical language and symbols	_____	_____	_____

MATHEMATICAL DISPOSITION

	Substantial Growth	Some Growth	No Growth
1. Has confidence in ability to do mathematics	_____	_____	_____
2. Takes risks exploring mathematical ideas and trying alternatives	_____	_____	_____
3. Perseveres in mathematics activities	_____	_____	_____
4. Is interested in doing mathematics	_____	_____	_____

© Addison-Wesley Publishing Company, Inc.